IMMIGRATION
THEN AND NOW

Background Information
Audiotape • Literature Links
Poster • Activities

by Karen Baicker

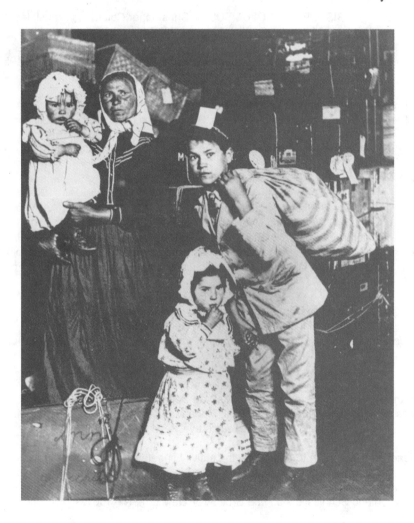

SCHOLASTIC
PROFESSIONAL BOOKS

NEW YORK • TORONTO • LONDON • AUCKLAND • SYDNEY

Dedication

For Paul, Jake, and Lucy
and my parents

ACKNOWLEDGMENTS

Many thanks to Virginia Dooley for her patience, friendship, and excellent editing. Thanks also to Janet Levine of the Ellis Island Oral History Project, and Michael Peros for his play.

Excerpt from THE LOG OF CHRISTOPHER COLUMBUS by Christopher Columbus (translated by Robert H. Fuson), Camden, Maine: International Marine Publishing Company, 1987.

WHEN I FIRST CAME TO THIS LAND, words and music by Oscar Brand. TRO © Copyright 1957 (Renewed), 1965 (Renewed) Ludlow Music, Inc., New York, NY. Used by permission.

I, TOO from Selected Poems of Langston Hughes. Copyright 1926 by Alfred A. Knopf Inc. and renewed 1954 by Langston Hughes. Reprinted by permission of publisher.

THE GREATEST TABLE written and edited by Michael Rosen, Harcourt Brace & Company, New York, New York, 1994.

PHOTO CREDITS

Cover: by Lewis Hine, A/P Wide World Photos
Interior: p. 1, 11, 14, 16, 31, 32, 35: A/P Wide World Photos; p. 5, 36, 71: Paul Sakuma for A/P Wide World Photos; p. 41 and 68: Marty Ledenhandler for A/P Wide World Photos; p. 9: Library of Congress; p. 17: Port of New York Authority
Poster: Jamestown and ship: Library of Congress; Ellis Island and "Registering Emigrants": Museum of the City of New York; citizenship ceremony: Paul Sakuma for A/P Wide World; Chinese school: Archive Photos; slave ship: Schomburg Center for Research in Black Culture, The New York Public Library, Astor, Lenox, and Tilden Foundations

AUDIOTAPE CREDITS

Executive Producer, Consultant, and Narrator: Bill Gordh
Musical Arrangements: George Wurzbach
Special thanks to Lu Yu of ARTS, Inc., New York City; Amy Ng; Iliana Oviedo Toledo, and Brent Tupa.

Cover design by Jaime Lucero and Vincent Ceci
Text and interior and poster design by Melinda Belter for Boultinghouse & Boultinghouse
Illustrations by Kate Flanagan, Tony Caldwell, Mona Mark, Rosiland Solomon, and Melinda Belter
Photo Research by Cheryl Moch

Kit ISBN 0-590-93097-4
Book ISBN 0-590-36055-8
Copyright © 1997 Karen Baicker
All rights reserved.
Printed in the U.S.A.

21 20 19 18 17 16 15 14 13   8 9/9 0/0

TABLE OF CONTENTS

UNIT 3

LIBERTY AND JUSTICE FOR ALL

INTRODUCTION

For centuries, people have been coming to America to make new lives for themselves and their children. They have come for many reasons—economic, social, political. Many thought they would find streets literally paved with gold. In fact, their adventures were postmarked with pain: the trauma of leaving their loved ones, the arduous journey, and difficult adjustments upon arrival. Frequently they faced poverty and discrimination in their new homes.

And yet, the prospect of immigration has continued to be filled with optimism and excitement. And the ultimate goal of immigrants to our country—United States citizenship—is still full of promise. While immigrants come from diverse backgrounds with varied motives, they generally share the characteristics of courage, determination, ambition, and the ability to overcome hardship through energy and hard work.

Today, we are bombarded with statistics about the changing face of America. The face of our classrooms is changing as well, bringing new, challenging issues to the forefront. How do we best address the increasing diversity of our student population? How do we discuss the challenges that immigration poses to the nation?

The first step is to build awareness of the history of immigration in our country. This book will help you provide students with an overview of the role of immigration in building our country—from the time Native Americans crossed the Bering Strait,

through the first arrival of European explorers and the massive waves of immigrants to follow, to the complexities of today's demographics. Through literature, primary sources, and hands-on activities, students will come to an understanding of the difficulties and issues that have confronted our nation's newcomers.

Students will also explore the variety of cultures today and how they have contributed to the complexion of our nation. Those who are ready will have the opportunity to explore broader, national issues such as immigration laws, economic impact, illegal immigration, and discrimination. They will explore the balance between assimilation and maintaining cultural identity.

The group activities have been designed to foster tolerance, understanding, and learning. Throughout this book you will find "Talking Points" features which invite discussion of current immigration topics. Many of these difficult issues require careful treatment. Your own sensitivity to the dynamics in your classroom and to your students' backgrounds is an essential component of this program.

One of the most important things you can teach about immigration is respect for the diversity of our cultures. It is also important for students to gain an understanding of what unites us as American citizens. The final unit of this book is dedicated to that purpose, to emphasizing the aspects of citizenship that bring all Americans together.

LAND OF PROMISE

OUR IMMIGRANT HERITAGE

Everyone in your classroom can trace a relative who arrived, yesterday or centuries ago, as an immigrant. They may have come by boat or by plane, for money or for love, but they faced many of the same circumstances. The following activities will help students recognize their common heritage and distinct backgrounds.

ACTIVITY

We're All Connected

Use this activity to demonstrate visually the connections we have with different countries and with each other. For this activity you'll need the following items:

- a large wall map of the world or an overhead projector and a world map transparency

- a bulletin board

- push pins

- different colors of yarn

- paper plates or photographs of students

Teaching Tip
You may want to color code the yarn according to country or world region.

Place a large map of the world on a bulletin board. Or, use a transparency to project and trace a map onto a bulletin board.

Have students make representations of themselves. They can make faces using small paper plates. Or, you can use photographs of the students. Place the pictures around the outside edges of the map.

Students should then take pieces of yarn and stretch them from their pictures to different countries of their ancestry. Attach them using pushpins. After students have completed the activity, take a look at the resulting web—a nice, graphic demonstration of our varied heritage.

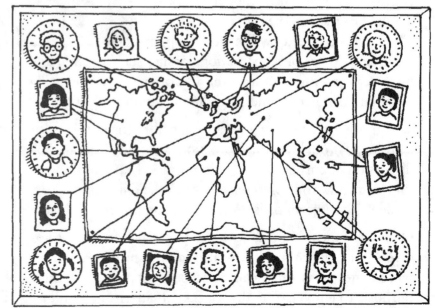

Extend It! Your class may want to try a domino-type exercise to further explore our connections with each other. One student can stand next to another if they share a country from their past. See if they can achieve a full circle around the classroom. (Example: Susan has Irish and German roots; she can stand next to Peter who has German and Russian roots; he can stand next to Lise who has Russian and Asian roots, etc.)

ACTIVITY
Heritage Time Line

Use the **poster** included in this book to create an overview of the history of immigration in our country. Point out that while our nation has been built by immigrants, people have come for many different reasons. Ask students to brainstorm what some of the reasons might have been, keeping a list on the chalkboard. Some, such as enslaved Africans, came against their will. You can sort the reasons behind the decision to immigrate into broad categories, such as personal, economic, political, social, and religious.

Display the **poster** on a wall. If students know their ancestry, have them put stickers or post-its on the part of the time line that shows when their relatives came here. Point out that the influx of immigrants to our country has been fairly continuous, but not at constant levels.

ACTIVITY
The Great Wave Line

Have students use the template on page 21 to create a different kind of time line, one that reflects waves of immigration. Reproduce the wave and have students cut out copies so that the pieces will fit together like a jigsaw puzzle. You may prefer to copy the template onto oak tag for sturdiness. Ask students to work in groups to collect information. Do not try to force the time line to fit together in a smooth time sequence. There will be overlaps, with different country groupings.

- 1840s
- Irish + German
- fleeing poverty + war
- Chinese/Gold Rush

- 1880-1914
- Eastern Europe + Southern Europe
- 20 million
- economic opportunity
- freedom

- 1924-1965
- Restrictions
- fewer immigrants

Extend It! You may want to size the waves larger or smaller with a copy machine to reflect the extent of the wave. Make sure when you cut them out, however, that the jigsaw parts are still the same size.

Further Reading: *Coming to America*, by Betsy Maestro
New York: Scholastic, 1996.

Just for Fun: After you display the completed version, have students "do the wave" to celebrate the success of their cooperative effort!

COMING TO AMERICA

When explorers from Europe came to North America, Indians had been living here for many years. The following literature and primary source pieces will help students view Columbus's arrival as an early immigrant experience. Encourage them to view the encounter from both Columbus's perspective and that of the people he met.

LITERATURE LINK

Encounter
by Jane Yolen
San Diego: Harcourt Brace & Company, 1992.

Background Information: The picture book *Encounter* portrays the arrival of Christopher Columbus from the Native Americans' point of view. In an Author's Note at the end of this book, Jane Yolen writes: "Since most stories about that first encounter are from Columbus's point of view, I thought it would interest readers to hear a Taino boy speak. We don't have an actual record of that, so I have recreated what he might have said—using historical records and the storyteller's imagination."

Discuss with students the fact that the phrase "nation of immigrants" has negative connotations to some Native Americans. Native Americans were immigrants as well, traveling across the Bering Strait over 20,000 years ago. But in another sense, they were the first people here and those who followed were immigrants.

Reading Aloud
Have students take turns reading the text to this story aloud. Discuss which parts may stem from research and which parts come from the author's and illustrator's imaginations.

Freeze Frame
Have students reenact the first encounter between Christopher Columbus and his group and the Taino. While they are acting, stop them periodically by saying, "Freeze." Then tap someone on the shoulder. That

Teaching Tip
During the Freeze Frame activity, observe students' perceptions of Native Americans. Unfortunately, some may have picked up stereotypes, and this is a good opportunity to dispel them. Point out that there were and are many different Native American groups, with different languages and cultures. Be on the watch for war cries, feathered headbands, and terms such as "savage." Educate students about Native American cultures today, which, except on special occasions, are largely the same as other American cultures.

person should describe how he or she is feeling. Continue this exercise until both sides have been thoroughly explored.

Dream Catcher

Dreams are very significant in the culture of many Native American groups. In *Encounter* the Taino boy pays close attention to the signals in his dreams. Another Native American group, the Ojibwa, believed that the air at night is full of dreams. They wove "dream catchers" and hung them in their homes. The catchers would dangle in the air and catch dreams as they drifted by. Good dreams would elude the catchers and slide down the feather to the sleeping people. Bad dreams would get tangled in the web and disappear with daybreak.

Help your students make their own dream catchers. Take a small, supple branch, such as a willow branch, and form it into a circle. Tie with a string. You can use leather, string, or even waxed dental floss. Form a web by weaving in and out and across the circle. Secure a feather and some beads or stones in the middle of the catcher. Display the dream catcher in the classroom—or let students hang them above their beds at home.

The Log of Christopher Columbus

by Christopher Columbus (translated by Robert H. Fuson)
Camden, ME: International Marine Publishing Company, 1987.

Read part of Columbus's journal out loud, to contrast the points of view of the Taino and Columbus. As you read and discuss this excerpt, draw parallels to the different perspectives that have always existed between immigrants and current residents, and that continue to exist today.

Discuss the fact that the explorers' journals are widely available, while little exists detailing the perspectives of the Native Americans. Here is an excerpt you can use, from Columbus's journal. This entry was made on October 12th, the day we celebrate as Columbus Day.

At dawn we saw. . . people, and I went ashore in the ship's boat, armed. . .. I unfurled the royal banner and the captains brought the flags. . .. No sooner had we concluded the formalities of taking possession of the island, than people began to come to the beach. . .. All those that I saw were young people, none of whom was over 30 years old. They are very well-built people, with handsome bodies and very fine faces. . .. Their eyes are large and very pretty. . .. These are tall people and their legs. . . are quite straight. Their hair is straight, and coarse like horsehair. They wear it short over

the eyebrows, but they have a long hank in the back that they never cut. Many of the natives paint their faces; others paint their whole bodies. . ..

The people here called this island Guanahani in their language, and their speech is very fluent, although I do not understand any of it. They are friendly and well-dispositioned people who bear no arms except for small spears. . .. They traded and gave everything they had with good will, but it seems to me that they have very little and are poor in everything. . ..

This afternoon the people. . . came swimming to our ships and in boats made from one log. They brought us parrots, balls of cotton thread, spears, and many other things. . .. For these items we swapped them little glass beads and hawks' bells. . ..

They ought to make good and skilled servants, for they repeat very quickly whatever we say to them. . ... I will take six of them to Your Highness when I depart. . ..

TALKING POINTS People have long celebrated October 12th as Columbus Day. But in recent years, people have begun to question the holiday. Did Columbus and his group mistreat the Native Americans they encountered during their explorations? Does the day in fact mark a loss for Native Americans and their culture? Or, did these brave explorers contribute to the growth of our country and to the knowledge of the world at the time? Discuss these issues with your students. Have them think of a way to mark the encounter that would honor both cultures.

ELLIS ISLAND
THE GOLDEN DOOR OR ISLAND OF TEARS?

Immigrants have come to the United States through many different ports. They have come through Angel Island, through Galveston, New Orleans, Boston, Seattle, Detroit, and other cities. But one port of entry has become synonymous with immigration to the United States. That place is Ellis Island.

F•Y•I

Almost half of all Americans today have a relative who came through Ellis Island.

From 1892 to 1954, this 27 1/2 acre patch of land in New York Bay was the main station through which hopeful newcomers were filtered. For the first 30 years after opening, 90 percent of all immigrants came through Ellis Island. In staggering numbers they came from over 50 countries in jam-packed boats. Each passenger was given a numbered tag. As they arrived and walked through the immigration station, officials with lists waited, watched, and judged.

Applicants were monitored for contagious diseases or other health problems. They were asked about job prospects, money, and their ultimate destinations. This process was very intimidating for most immigrants, who had frequently just survived a horrific journey. In fact, over 98 percent of all applicants were ultimately admitted. Here's a look at some other interesting facts that may help your students gain a better understanding of the role of Ellis Island:

- Between 1892-1924, 16 million people passed through the immigration station.

- After waiting in long lines, the questioning was fast and furious—immigrants were asked approximately 30 questions in a two-minute period.

- After being admitted, approximately one third went on to live in New York City.

- By 1914, the immigration station had almost become a city unto itself, complete with 33 buildings, including a chapel, hospital, laundry room, waiting room, dormitory, money exchange, post office, and restaurants.

Better than all of these statistics, however, are actual photographs, diaries, and oral histories documenting this national experience. In 1954, Ellis Island was closed as an immigration station, and the buildings were virtually abandoned. In 1990, after a seven-year renovation project, the Ellis Island Immigration Museum was opened. Today, over 2 million visitors a year go to try to imagine what life was like for immigrants long ago. Many of them are looking for information about their own ancestors.

AUDIOTAPE Your students can listen to some actual Ellis Island oral histories on the audiotape.

ACTIVITY ### First Stop, Ellis Island! A Play
Your students may enjoy reading aloud the play on pages 22-28 about immigrants arriving at Ellis Island. Reading aloud or performing a play is a very effective way to make history come alive.

If you choose a read-aloud format, encourage students to spend a few moments "getting acquainted" with their characters by reading over their lines.

For a more elaborate performance, students may want to create scenery and props, dress in costumes, and conduct several rehearsals. Invite other classes and/or parents to attend the performance.

TALKING POINTS In the play, the issue of citizenship by birth is central to the second act. The 14th Amendment, passed in 1866, provided that "all persons born . . . in the United States" were automatically citizens. Now, over 130 years later, that amendment has come under fire. Some people believe that children born to illegal immigrants do not have the right to United States citizenship. Barbara Jordan, former chairwoman of the United States Commission on Immigration Reform, criticized the proposal one month before her death in 1996: "To deny birthright citizenship is to derail the engine of American liberty." Help your students research the pros and cons, and debate the issue.

Leaving Home

ACTIVITY

Deciding to come to America was not an easy decision for immigrants. It generally involved spending all of their savings. It also usually meant separation from their family, friends, and home. They could take very little with them, as space was precious on board the ships. They had to pay by size and weight of their bundles. Help your students imagine what these decisions were like, and practice their own decision-making skills with this activity.

Each student should use a pillowcase brought from home. Tell them that they can fill the pillowcase with whatever they choose, not to exceed a specified weight amount (say, ten pounds). Tell them to consider the following items for inclusion: things they will need on the trip; things that will remind them of their homes and family; food items; things they might want when they get to America.

Students can actually do this exercise at home and bring in their bundles. Alternatively, they can write or draw the objects on slips of paper and place them in their sacks. Have them share the contents, and the decision-making process, with each other. Make this exercise more relevant by showing them photographs of immigrants with their real-life bundles and reading their descriptions of what they brought. (See Primary Source Link: *Immigrant Kids* (page 13) and the Further Reading list (page 15) to help find these sources.)

The Journey

ACTIVITY

Use photographs again to show students what the boats were like. Passengers were crowded together in unhealthy conditions. The stench was often overpowering, from seasick passengers, rotten food, and other unsanitary conditions. Nonetheless, people had their eyes set for New York Harbor.

For this activity, use masking tape to section off a 6-foot by 4-foot rectangle in your classroom or on the playground. (Adjust the space according to the number of students in your class.) If you have done the Leaving Home activity, have students carry their bundles with them. One by one, they may enter the "boat." Have them sit down, but tell them they must stay completely within the marked off area. Once the area is very crowded, call on students to try to do certain activities: remove a sweater, pass a note to a classmate in a different corner, take a shoe off, etc. While they are in this situation, read some primary source descriptions of the boat rides. Is anyone starting to get uncomfortable? Antsy? Claustrophobic? Discuss their feelings, and encourage them to imagine what the journey would have been like.

Just for Fun: If you want to extend the simulation, you could set up a fan and shoot water from a spray bottle on the "boat!"

The Arrival

Recreate the examination process in your classroom. Ask several volunteers to become inspectors with you. Other students should wait in chairs, in the "waiting room." Call the immigrants up individually. Watch the way they walk. Then make notes. The student inspectors ask rapid-fire questions of the "immigrants." Here are some sample questions: What is your name? What is your birthday? Name the members of your family. What country are you from? Are you ill? Have you ever been in prison? Hospitalized? What do you plan to do for work? How much money do you have? How did you get that money? Where will you live? Whom will you live with?

F•Y•I

In the 1800s, as many as one in ten passengers died during the journey. Many more became seriously ill.

Teaching Tip

You might try asking the questions in a foreign language (or get someone who speaks a foreign language to do so for you). Point out that frequently the immigrants spoke little English, so the questioning process was even more frightening.

PRIMARY SOURCE

Immigrant Kids
by Russell Freedman
New York: Dutton, 1980.

Quite possibly the best book available of this kind, *Immigrant Kids* contains primary sources, photographs, and descriptions of what immigration was like for children arriving in the late 1800s and around the turn of the century. Many of them lived in poverty and worked in sweatshops. But they also played baseball in the streets, chased ice cream vendors, and gained "a taste for the wonderful freedom their parents had come to America to find." The photographs are by Lewis Hine, Jacob Riis, and other famous immigrant photographers. Share the following and other excerpts with your class:

> My first impressions of the New World will always remain etched in my memory, particularly that hazy October morning when I first saw Ellis Island. The steamer Florida, fourteen days out of Naples, filled to capacity with 1600 natives of Italy, had weathered one of the worst storms in our captain's memory; and glad we were, both children and grown-ups, to leave the open sea. . .. My mother, my stepfather, my brother Giuseppe, and my two sisters, Liberta and Helvetia, all of us together, happy that we had come through the storm safely, clustered on the foredeck for fear of separation and looked with wonder on this miraculous land of our dreams. . .. Jabbered conversation, sharp cries, laughs and cheers—a steady din filled the air. Mothers and fathers lifted up babies so that they too could see, off to the left, the Statue of Liberty.
>
> —Edward Corsi

Note to your students that Edward Corsi, who was ten years old at the time he describes (1907), later became United States Commissioner of Immigration!

A Thousand Words

The preface to *Immigrant Kids* describes the photographers and their techniques. Photography at the time was a new technology, and small, hand-held cameras the newest development. Known as "detective cameras," photographers were able for the first time to take pictures unobtrusively.

Invite students to study some of the photographs in this book. Encourage them to play detectives themselves, deducing clues about the lives and personalities of the people depicted. Then ask them to bring in or take photographs that show as much as possible about their own lives.

> ### Teaching Tip
> Many of the photographs were taken from Jacob Riis' famous book, How the Other Half Lives (1890). Others were taken by Lewis Hine, who later led a crusade to change some of the conditions he documented.

I Was Dreaming to Come to America
edited by Veronica Lawlor
New York: Viking, 1995.

The Ellis Island Oral History Project began in 1973 with some interviews with people who had immigrated through Ellis Island. The project has grown, and there are now over 1,400 interviews on tape.

F • Y • I

The first immigrant to land at Ellis Island and set foot in the processing center was a 15-year-old girl from Ireland, in 1892. Her name was Annie Moore.

Going to America then was almost like going to the moon. . . . We were all bound for places about which we knew nothing at all and for a country that was totally strange to us.

Golda Meir
Russia
arrived in 1906 • Age 8

Most dear to me are the shoes my mother wore when she first set foot on the soil of America. . ... She landed in America in those shoes and somehow or other she felt that she was going to hang on to them. They are brown high-top shoes that had been soled and resoled and stitched and mended in Sweden to hold them together 'til she could get to America. We just kept them. And then. . ... as I grew up and everything, I said, "Don't ever throw them away."

Brigitta Hedman Fischter
Sweden
arrived in 1924 • Age 6

My father's dream and prayer always was "I must get my family to America. . .." America was paradise. The streets were covered with gold. And when we arrived here, and when we landed from Ellis Island and [went] to Buffalo, it was as if God's great promise had been fulfilled that we would eventually find freedom.

Vartan Harunian
Turkey (Armenia)
arrived in 1922 • Age 7

The Oral History Library is a great resource. For more information, contact the Ellis Island Oral History Project, Ellis Island Immigration Museum, New York, New York 10004.

ACTIVITY ## Interviews

What questions would students like to ask immigrants who passed through Ellis Island? Ask students to make lists. Then have them work in pairs to pose and respond to each others' questions.

Further Reading: *If Your Name Was Changed at Ellis Island* by Ellen Levine New York, Scholastic, 1993.

Ellis Island: New Hope in a New Land by William Jay Jacobs, New York: Charles Scribner's Sons, 1990.

ANGEL ISLAND

Background Information: Sometimes known as the "Ellis Island of the West," Angel Island served as the point of entry for many immigrants for 30 years. Unlike Ellis Island, however, the immigration station also served as a detention center, or temporary prison, for thousands of Chinese immigrants. In 1882, the United States passed its first immigration restriction law, the Chinese Exclusion Act. The law was passed out of discrimination and fear, specifically to limit Chinese immigration.

F • Y • I
Between 1910 and 1940, over 175,000 Chinese passed through Angel Island.

The result was Angel Island, which opened in 1910 off the coast of San Francisco. As ships arrived in San Francisco's harbor, immigration officials directed most Chinese immigrants to Angel Island. They were separated from their families, made to wait long periods of time, and were then subjected to an interrogation process. The lucky ones waited a few weeks until their fate was determined. Some waited almost two years.

They waited in crowded living quarters, separated from their families, passing the days with enforced routines. The anxiety of waiting for the interrogation built. While they were waiting, many relieved the stress by writing poems, like the one below, on the wooden barracks walls. They carved them, or used pencils, or paint and brushes. One way or another, they found relief by expressing their emotions.

The station was closed in 1940 when a fire destroyed many of the buildings. In 1943, the Chinese Exclusion Act was repealed. Fortunately, the poems were discovered by a United States Park Ranger in 1970 before they were demolished. Thousands of school children visit the Angel Island Immigration Station every year, where they can still read poems on the barracks walls.

埃崙此地為仙島
山野原來是監牢
既望張網焉投入
祇為囊空莫奈何

Writing Poems

Reproduce the poems on page 29 to share with your students. Have students read the selections aloud. Then encourage students to explore how the detainees must have felt by writing their own poems.

Further Reading: *Tales from Gold Mountain: Stories of the Chinese in the New World* by Paul Yee
New York: Macmillan, 1989.

Angel Island Prisoner: 1922 by Helen Chetin
Berkeley, CA: New Seed Press, 1982.

STATUE OF LIBERTY

The Statue of Liberty was a gift from the people of France, to celebrate the one hundredth anniversary of the Declaration of Independence. The statue arrived in over 200 crates. Here's how a reporter from *The World* described what he saw:

In a case were the nose, eyes, and mouth. . .. In another, the eyebrows and fore-head. The left ear, some pieces of hair, and the crown of the head were in a case ten by twenty feet. Another case, eight feet long, held one of her curls.

It's no wonder that the statue arrived almost ten years late! Share some of these facts and figures with your students before introducing some of the concepts behind "Lady Liberty."

- The base of the statue alone weighs 3,500 tons. That's equal to the weight of 3,900 elephants!

- Just one fingernail on the statue is over a foot long—13 inches by 10 inches.

- To reach the observation deck visitors can climb 335 steps, to just inside the crown. Or they can take an elevator from the ground to the top of the base, and walk the remaining 168 steps.

- Her nose is about as long as you are tall!

- The seven spikes on her crown represent the seven continents and the seven seas.

A committee of people in our country raised money to build the pedestal and armature, but fell short of the needed amount. Joseph Pulitzer's newspaper, *The World*, solicited contributions. School children joined adults all over the country and raised $100,000 in 1885, to complete the project.

The New Colossus

Show your students the poem and cartoon on page 30 to discuss the changes in immigration policy since the donation of the Statue of Liberty. Use the opportunity to discuss political cartoons. Do students think they are an effective way to communicate points of view? What is the cartoonist trying to say about our immigration policies? Ask students to clip other political cartoons and try to explain their meaning. Ask them to state an opinion and then make a cartoon to illustrate that point. Students can listen to the poem "The New Colossus" on the audiotape.

AUDIOTAPE

Further Reading: *How They Built the Statue of Liberty*, by Mary J. Shapiro New York: Random House, 1995.

VOICES

It's one thing to read all of the facts about the history of immigration in our country. But the best knowledge comes from listening to the words of real immigrants. Fortunately, there are many diaries of children and adults, and many photographs that help us take a peek into the lives of immigrants.

 **Mini-Anthology**

Make copies of pages 31-37 for students. As they read this mini-anthology, ask them to think about their own lives. Have they ever moved somewhere new? How did it feel? Encourage them to write responses to the anthology selections as journal entries.

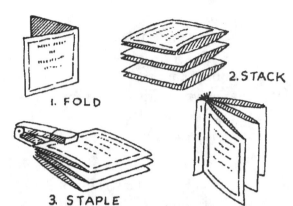

1. FOLD
2. STACK
3. STAPLE

L I T E R A T U R E   L I N K

The Always Prayer Shawl
by Sheldon Oberman
Honesdale, PA: Boyds Mill Press, 1994.

Background Information: This is a fictional picture book, but it is based on the life of the author's grandfather. Sheldon Oberman was preparing for his son Adam's bar mitzvah when he came across his grandfather's prayer shawl. His grandfather had brought the shawl with him when he emigrated from Russia. The discovery inspired this story, as a bar mitzvah gift from the author to his son.

The Story: Adam is a young Jewish boy living in czarist Russia. He must flee his country at the outbreak of the Russian Revolution. Before he sets sail for his new land, his grandfather gives him a prayer shawl that was handed to him by his own grandfather, who was also named Adam. Adam grows up and his world changes. He learns English and lives in an apartment—but throughout these changes "the Always Prayer Shawl" offers him constancy and a sense of tradition. When Adam has his own grandson, he passes the prayer shawl on once again.

Pass It On

The theme of this book is the passing of objects and traditions from generation to generation. Invite students to find an object in their own homes that has some tradition, history, or meaning to their family. Have them create time lines and maps tracing the history of the object. Then ask students to write descriptions of what the object symbolizes to them about their families and about tradition.

You might also use the opportunity to explore Bat and Bar Mitzvah ceremonies, which Jewish boys and girls participate in when they turn 13 years old. Ask students to compare these ceremonies with other practices celebrating growing up.

Further Reading: *The Whispering Cloth*, by Pegi Deitz Shea
Honesdale, PA: Boyds Mills Press, 1995.

L I T E R A T U R E   L I N K

When I First Came to This Land
by Oscar Brand
New York: G. P. Putnam's Sons, 1965.

In 1948, Oscar Brand, a well-known folk singer was asked to write a song about immigrants coming to this country. He wanted to describe the challenges they faced as they tried to develop the land, and the simple pleasures they found through their hard work. *When I First Came to This Land* became a hit, making its way across the country. In 1957 a picture book was published, illustrating the humorous and simple lyrics. The book has been reissued several times, but is currently out-of-print. You can still find it in many libraries, and it has high appeal for children.

AUDIOTAPE The words to *When I First Came to This Land* are on the student reproducible on page 38. Invite students to sing along with the tape.

CONTRIBUTIONS

The activities that follow will give students some sense of the huge impact immigrants have had on American culture. Encourage them to think about food and traditions that have been brought to the United States from other countries.

ACTIVITY

Word Maps
One way to get a sense of the contributions and impact of different immigrant groups is to take a look at our language. By tracing the way certain words came into American English, students can learn about the different groups that came here and the impact they had when they arrived.

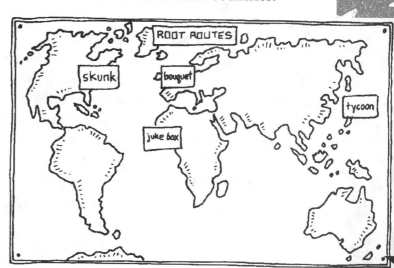

Write the words in the lists below on index cards. Distribute the cards to small groups of students. Explain to students that dictionaries show the etymology, or origins of words. You may want to make a list of the country codes and put them on the chalkboard for students. Have them work in groups, using dictionaries to try to trace the origin of the words. They should fill in the country of origin, and any other information they come across. Next, have students tape the index cards onto a large wall map of the world. Make a title for the map: ROOT ROUTES. Place the title at the top of the map.

abalone [Spanish]	honcho [Japanese]	prairie [French]
alligator [Spanish]	hurricane [Taino/ Spanish]	raccoon [Powhatan]
banjo [Kimbundu-Angola]	jazz [W. African]	reindeer [Scandinavian]
blouse [French]	juke box [W. African]	skunk [Massachusett]
boondocks [Tagalog]	knife [German]	smithereens [Irish]
bouquet [French]	leprechaun [Irish]	succotash [Native American]
caribou [Micmac]	macinaw [Ojibwa]	toboggan [Micmac]
carousel [French]	mosquito [Portuguese]	tomato [Spanish]
chef [French]	noodles [German]	trombone [Italian]
chipmunk [Algonkian]	omelet [French]	trousers [Irish]
cocoa [Spanish]	pastrami [Yiddish]	tycoon [Japanese/ Chinese]
coffee [Turkish]	patio [Spanish]	violin [Italian]
cookie [Dutch]	pickle [Dutch]	waffle [Dutch]
crag [Welsh]	podunk [New England Algonkian]	yen [Chinese]
Dachshund [German]	poodle [German]	
gung-ho [Chinese]	powwow [Narragansett]	
hamburger [German]		

Extend It! Have students find other words that came into American English through the arrival of immigrants.

Famous Immigrants

ACTIVITY

Use the reproducibles on pages 39 and 40 to introduce your students to some famous American immigrants who have made great contributions to our culture. For example, students may be interested to know that *God Bless America* was written by immigrant Irving Berlin. Encourage them to add the names of other immigrants to the list.

Further Reading: *By the Dawn's Early Light*, by Steven Kroll New York: Scholastic, 1994.

Our National Anthem, by Stephanie St. Pierre, Brookfield, CT: The Millbrook Press, 1992.

Name_____

The Great Wave Line

Cut out the wave. Work with the other members of your group to collect information on different immigrant groups to complete the wave.

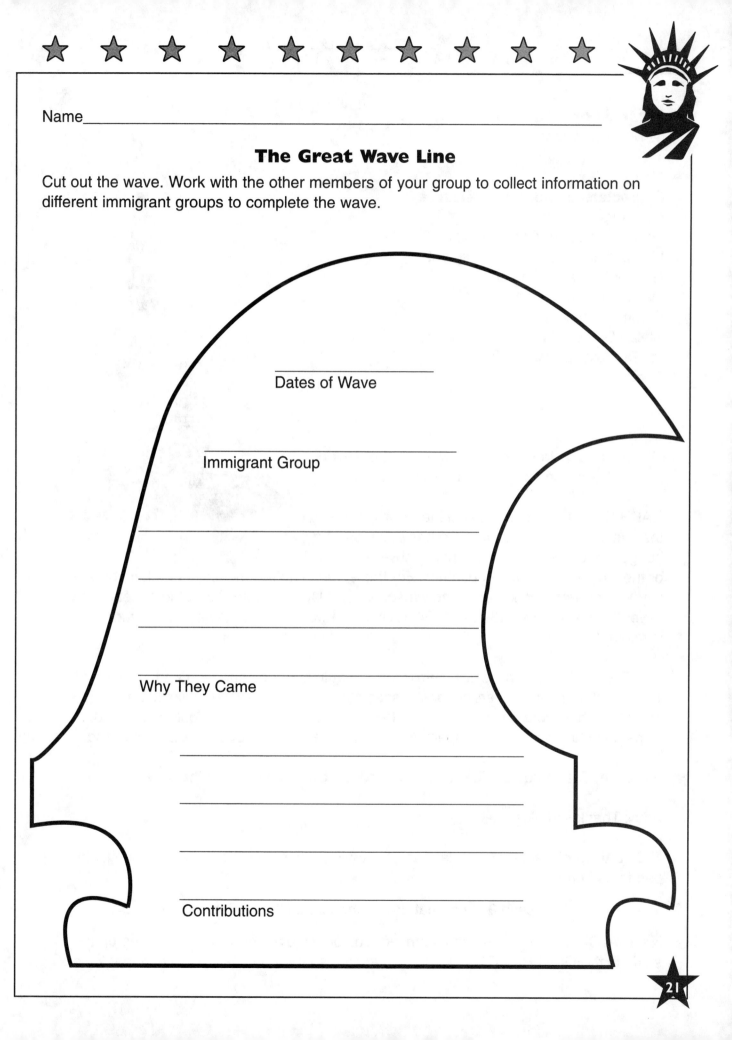

_____

Dates of Wave

_____

Immigrant Group

_____

_____

_____

Why They Came

_____

_____

_____

Contributions

First Stop, Ellis Island!
by Michael Peros

Characters (in order of appearance)
Narrators 1 and 2
Paulina Spigos: a Greek immigrant
Ivan Erdman: a Russian immigrant
Nicolai Erdman: Ivan's son
Inspectors 1-4
Commissioner Curran
Stefan Brodsky: a Polish American
Ida Brodsky: Stefan's wife
Doctor

ACT 1
Scene I: 1912. In New York Harbor, on the deck of
a barge approaching Ellis Island.

NARRATOR 1: Millions of people left Europe during
the late 1800s. They fled their homes because of
hunger, religious persecution, harsh governments,
or the lack of jobs in their countries. For these immigrants, America was a land of opportunity. Wages were higher, and land was cheaper. Many had heard that the streets were paved with gold! From 1892 to 1954, Ellis Island was the first stop in America for many immigrants.

NARRATOR 2: Meet three new immigrants—Paulina Spigos and Ivan and Nicolai Erdman. They've already been checked for illnesses such as yellow fever, smallpox, and typhus. The ships they were on stopped in the lower part of the bay. Then doctors boarded the ships and checked the passengers. Now they're being taken by barge to Ellis Island.

PAULINA: The Statue of Liberty. . . she's so beautiful! Can you see the lady?

IVAN: Thank you, yes.

NICOLAI (to his father): America! Everything will be fine now. Nothing bad will ever happen to us here!

Scene 2: Later that day. In the Great Hall on Ellis Island.

NARRATOR 1: As the immigrants arrived, doctors studied the way they walked up the stairs to the Great Hall. (This was known as the "six-second medical.") Then the doctors

would do a more thorough exam. After that, inspectors asked the immigrants a series of questions. Chances were—if you were a man in good health, with no criminal record and good prospects for employment—you'd be allowed to enter America within a few hours.

NARRATOR 2: The rules, however, were more strict for women who were traveling alone, like Paulina.

INSPECTOR 1: Your full name is Paulina Spigos?

PAULINA: Yes, sir, Paulina Spigos. I'm from Greece.

INSPECTOR 1: The doctors tell me you're in good health. You're single?

PAULINA: I'm engaged to Spiros Paniotis of Chicago.

INSPECTOR 1: Uh-huh. And you know this Spiros Paniotis of Chicago?

PAULINA (*indignant, but nervous*): Of course I know him. I grew up with him. He came here two years ago with his parents. He says he is ready for me to join him. Here, it says so in this letter.

INSPECTOR 1: Do I look like I can read Greek? He's meeting you here?

PAULINA: No, Chicago is too far away. He works.

INSPECTOR 1: Uh-huh. Since Chicago is too far away, how will you get there?

PAULINA: I have money for a train ticket.

INSPECTOR 1: Uh-huh. Okay, Miss Spigos, only a few more questions: How much is five plus five?

PAULINA: Ten.

INSPECTOR 1: How do you wash stairs? From the top or from the bottom?

PAULINA: With all respect sir, I did not come to America to wash stairs.

INSPECTOR 1: I see. Your Spiros is rich, is he? You'll have someone washing the stairs for you? Is that what your Spiros has told you? You see, Miss Spigos this is exactly why we don't like to let women in by themselves.

PAULINA: I've known Spiros all my life. I know exactly what my life here in America will be like. Do you want to know what my life was like in Greece? Do you care that I had no family there?

INSPECTOR 1: Just calm down, Miss Spigos. We just don't want you falling into the wrong hands. But you seem like a woman who can take care of herself. Just be careful. You can change your money here for American dollars. You can buy your train ticket here, too. Next!

PAULINA: Inspector? The stairs? From the top to the bottom.

Scene 3: Same day. An inspector's office on Ellis Island.

NARRATOR 1: About twenty percent of all immigrants were held for further questioning. About two percent of these were sent back to their home countries. People could be denied entry into the United States for a number of reasons: if they had criminal records, medical problems, or if they might not be able to support themselves.

NARRATOR 2: Sometimes families traveled all the way to America, only to be separated.

INSPECTOR 3: Mr. Erdman, why have you come to the United States?

IVAN: We had to. It was very hard for us in Russia.

NICOLAI: Inspector, we are Jewish. Last year, our family was forced to move. My father found it harder to work.

INSPECTOR 3: What was your business, Mr. Erdman?

IVAN: I was a tailor.

INSPECTOR 3: How much did you earn?

IVAN: About ten to twelve rubles.

INSPECTOR 3: Hmmm . . . that's about three dollars a week. Nicolai, what kind of work do you do?

NICOLAI: I was a student—until the government said I couldn't go to school anymore.

INSPECTOR 3 (to Ivan): Do you have a job waiting for you?

IVAN: No, Inspector. We know that it is against the law to have a job waiting for us. But, well, my brother Leon is here. He is a tailor, also.

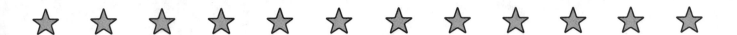

INSPECTOR 3: What does he earn?

IVAN: About twelve rubles—I mean, $12 a week.

INSPECTOR 3: Does he have a family?

IVAN: A wife and four children. (*Shifting weight from foot to foot, looking tired.*)

INSPECTOR 3: Our medical examiner says your fingers are stiff and swollen. You look like your legs hurt. You probably have arthritis.

IVAN: No, no, it's nothing. It's been a very long day.

INSPECTOR 3: Nicolai, what are your plans here in America?

NICOLAI: I am strong. There are many things I can do here. My father will be well taken care of.

INSPECTOR 3: You have $23 between you. Look at your father's hands—he can't work! And you—you have no job experience at all! Do you know how many strong, young men come into this country every day? I'm sorry. (*Marks the letters "SI" on the shoulder of Ivan's coat.*)

NICOLAI: "SI?" What does that stand for?

INSPECTOR 3: Special Inquiry. It means your father will be deported, sent back to Russia.

NICOLAI: But they will kill him! No, no, you can't send him back!

IVAN: Nicolai, do not say anything.

NICOLAI: Papa, I am not like you. I cannot say yes to everything. (*to the inspector*) I will take care of him. I will earn enough money for both of us to live.

INSPECTOR 3 (*shrugging*): Maybe you can convince the Board of Special Inquiry. Explain your situation to the inspectors there. They'll give you a translator if you need one. Then they will decide if your father can stay. Next!

(*Bewildered, Ivan and Nicolai leave the inspector's office.*)

IVAN: Well, Nicolai, I'm afraid we must say good-bye.

NICOLAI: Papa, no!

IVAN: We have talked to so many people these past few days. I'm tired. And look at my hands! They're right . . . I can't work the way I used to.

NICOLAI: Please, Papa, no! We will fight this. We will figure something out. You cannot go back to Russia.

IVAN: It is my home, son. Just as America will be yours. My mind is made up.

ACT 2
Scene 1, 1922. In the Great Hall of Ellis Island.

NARRATOR 1: Between 1901 and 1910, over seven million immigrants entered the United States through Ellis Island. The numbers dropped during World War I. But after the war ended in 1918, the numbers started rising. As a result, the First Quota Law was passed in 1921. This put a monthly limit on the number of immigrants who could enter the United States from any given country.

NARRATOR 2: Stefan Brodsky, a Polish-American man who immigrated to the United States two years earlier, is pacing in the Great Hall. Commissioner Curran, who is in charge of Ellis Island, approaches Stefan.

CURRAN: Good afternoon. Are you waiting for someone?

STEFAN: Yes, my wife Ida, Ida Brodsky. She's coming in from Poland. Her ship's a day late.

CURRAN: How long have you been in America?

STEFAN: Oh, we've both been here for two years. Ida only went back to visit her parents. Her mother's sick. I hope everything is all right.

CURRAN: No need to worry. I'm Commissioner Curran, and I can assure you that these little trips don't count against the Quota Law.

STEFAN: Thank you, Mr. Curran, but you don't understand—

CURRAN: You see, if your wife has already been admitted to the United States and then she goes back to her homeland, even if Poland's limit has been reached, she would probably be allowed in . . . (*Ida Brodsky, carrying a bundle, enters the Great Hall. She is accompanied by the ship's doctor and an inspector.*)

STEFAN: I realize that, but you—

IDA: Stefan!

STEFAN: Ida!

CURRAN: What's that she's carrying?!

STEFAN: I believe that's our baby. Excuse me, Commissioner. (*hurrying to Ida*)

IDA: Stefan, look—he has your eyes!

DOCTOR: Mrs. Brodsky needs to stay here in the hospital tonight so I can check her out. The baby was born just last night.

IDA: Stefan, there's a problem—

STEFAN: What? What is it? Are you all right? Is it the baby—-

IDA: No, nothing like that.

INSPECTOR 4: The Polish quota has been reached. To put it bluntly, the mother can stay, but the baby must leave.

IDA: Not my baby! I won't let it happen! Stefan, if our baby can't stay, I will return to Poland with him.

STEFAN: Commissioner, please help us.

INSPECTOR 4: Aboard ship, sir. On the *Lapland*, of the British Star Line.

CURRAN: Don't worry, Stefan. I'm sure we can work something out. (*to the inspector*) Where was the baby born?

CURRAN: There you are. The baby wasn't born in Poland, but on a British ship. The deck of a British ship, no matter where in the world it is, is the same as British soil. Include the baby in the British quota.

INSPECTOR 4: Sir. The British quota was reached yesterday.

IDA: Our baby can't come in?

CURRAN: Wait, wait! The baby was born on the *Lapland*? That ship's home port is Belgium. There! The baby is Belgian!

STEFAN: My baby is what?

INSPECTOR 4: I'm sorry, but the Belgian quota is also full.

CURRAN: Inspector, what are you trying to do here?

INSPECTOR 4: My job, Commissioner.

CURRAN: Listen, I think I've got it. You see with children, it's the way it is will wills. We follow the intention. It's clear enough that Ida was hurrying back so that the baby would be born in America. And the baby had the same intention—he wanted to be born in America. But the ship was a day late, and that upset everything. So, under the law, this baby, by intention, was born in America. This baby is American!

INSPECTOR 4 (*with a sigh*): All right. (*filling out a form*) Baby's name?

IDA (*whispering to Commissioner Curran*): What's your first name?

CURRAN: Kevin, ma'am. Kevin Curran.

IDA: Kevin, Inspector. (*Stefan and Ida link arms, and she passes the baby to her husband, beaming.*) Kevin Brodsky.

THE END

Name _____

The Poetry of Angel Island

These poems were found on barracks walls at Angel Island. After you read them, write your own poem about how detainees must have felt in the box below.

A prisoner in this wooden building, I am always sad and bored.
I remember since I left my native village, it has been several full moons.
The family at home is leaning on the door, urgently looking for letters.
Whom can I count on to tell them I am well?

Over a hundred poems are on the walls.
Looking at them, they are all pining at the delayed progress.
What can one sad person say to another?
Unfortunate travelers everywhere wish to commiserate . . . .
Since ancient times, heroes often were the first ones to
   face adversity.

埃崙此地爲仙島
山野原來是監牢
既望張綱焉投入
祇爲囊空莫奈何

I used to admire the land of the Flowery Flag as a country of abundance.
I immediately saved money and started my journey . . . .
I look up and see Oakland so close by.
I want to go back to my motherland to carry the farmer's hoe.
Discontent fills my belly and it is difficult for me to sleep.
I just write these few lines to express what is on my mind.

_____
_____
_____
_____
_____
_____

Name _____

Golden Door?

Emma Lazarus was a young poet from New York when she was asked to write a poem to be engraved on the pedestal of the Statue of Liberty. She wrote the poem, "The New Colossus," in 1883, to welcome people seeking freedom. What point do you think the cartoonist was trying to make? How do the thoughts expressed in the cartoon compare with those of Emma Lazarus? Use the back of this page to draw your own political cartoon.

The New Colossus

Not like the brazen giant of Greek fame,
With conquering limbs astride from land to land;
Here at our sea-washed sunset gates shall stand
A mighty woman with a torch, whose flame
Is the imprisoned lightning, and her name
Mother of Exiles. From her beacon-hand
Glows world-wide welcome; her mild eyes command
The air-bridged harbor that win cities fame.
Keep, ancient lands, your storied pomp! Cries she
With silent lips. "Give me your tired, your poor,
Your huddled masses yearning to breathe free,
The wretched refuse of your teeming shore.
Send these, the homeless, tempest-tost to me.
I lift my lamp beside the golden door!"

EMMA LAZARUS

IMMIGRANT VOICES

A MINI ANTHOLOGY

from
AN ALBUM OF THE GREAT WAVE OF IMMIGRATION

by April Koral
New York: Franklin Watts: 1992.

This book uses pictures and quotations to capture what life was like for those who immigrated during the "Great Wave." In these selections, two immigrants describe what it was like to leave their families behind.

Marcus Ravage
Russian immigrant

In the evening when we were alone together my mother would . . . gaze into my eyes as if she tried to absorb enough of me to last her for the coming months of absence. "You will write us, dear?" she kept asking continually . . . .

At the moment of departure, when the train drew into the station, she lost control of her feelings. As she embraced me for the last time her sobs became violent and father had to separate us. There was a despair in her way of clinging to me which I could not then understand. I understand it now. I never saw her again.

FOLD ↓

from
THE PROMISED LAND

by Mary Antin

Boston: The Atlantic Monthly Company, 1911.
(reprinted Boston: Houghton Mifflin Company, 1969.)

Many immigrants called America "the promised land." One of these hopeful immigrants was a 13-year-old Russian Jew named Mary Antin. In 1894, she immigrated to the United States. Later, she worked for women's rights, and became a poet and author. In 1911 she wrote an autobiography describing her immigration. She called it *The Promised Land.*

Mary Antin
Russian immigrant

So at last I was going to America! Really, really going at last! The boundaries burst. The arch of heaven soared. A million suns shone out for every star. The winds rushed in from outer space, roaring in my ears, "America! America!"

★ ★ ★

**An Italian immigrant
who left at age 22**

My heart aches every time I think about that afternoon when I left my parents and friends to go to the railroad station. My mother kissed me good-bye and then stood by the doorway stiff as a statue sobbing as my father and I left the house. At the station, even my father as hard as he tried could not keep the tears from filling his eyes.

WE CAME TO AMERICA

from

by Frances Cavanagh
Philadelphia: Macrae Smith Company, 1954

The editor of this book collected the firsthand accounts of immigrants who came to this country. She included information about why they came and what was going on in their countries during the times the immigrants left. This selection is by Lilly Daché, a woman who came from France in 1924 when she was just a teenager. She sold hats when she grew up, which later became very popular and chic. She wrote her biography in a book called *Talking Through My Hats.*

Lilly Daché
Teenage immigrant from France

I want to put down the things that have happened to Lilly Daché a redheaded French girl who traveled to America to seek her fortune— and found it. I want to put down the love I have for this big and busy and openhearted country. It was on a trip to Paris, when I was perhaps six or seven, that my dream of America first took

shape. In the same apartment house with us lived a small American girl of my own age named Olga White. She had fat sausage curls, and on them she wore big satin hair ribbons of pink or blue or white. She wore starched white dresses and white shoes and stockings. My sisters and I usually wore the checked gingham blouses and pinafores that were practically a uniform for French schoolgirls, and our shoes were black.

To me Olga seemed like a princess out of a fairy tale. She used to talk to me of America and the wonderful things to be found there. She said her family owned a real automobile and that she was allowed to have ice cream every Sunday.

Then and there I decided that my destiny was in America. I dreamed of the skyscrapers and the white shoes by night, and I planned practical means for the journey by day. I remembered that I had an uncle and some cousins living in America, and I decided that I would go and visit them . . . .

[Eleven years later, Lilly boarded a small, slow steamer and traveled for eleven days. She had studied hat making, and on the trip over she dreamed of skyscrapers, hat making, automobiles, and New York City. But when she arrived, the boat pulled into Hoboken, New Jersey, and Lilly was greatly disappointed at first. There were no skyscrapers, and she could not find her cousin. She settled in Philadelphia for a short time, but finally made her way to New York City.]

A yellow taxicab screamed to a stop not an inch behind me. The driver leaned out of the window and shook his fist at me "Jaywalker!" he shouted. "Wake up!"

I woke up, in the middle of a wild jump for the curb. I woke up with every sense tingling, and for the first time I looked around me.

There was a wonderful roar all around. It filled the air and pounded in my ears. I looked up and saw a train thundering above me on the elevated tracks. I looked down and felt the ground beneath my feet tremble and heard the muffled roar of subway trains below. I looked to my right and saw cars speeding north. I looked to my left and saw cars speeding south. In the middle of the street, trolley cars clanged and banged. On the sidewalks, men and women, boys and girls, made a lively, colorful, pushing throng.

"That'll teach you!" growled the taxi driver as he ground the gears of his cab.

I smiled at him and waved. I stood still, just where I was, in a narrow island in the middle of the wide street. I looked up at the towering buildings all around me. Here, then, were the skyscrapers! At last! Great stores. Tall office buildings . . . I drew a deep, intoxicating breath.

All at once I was fully awake, glad to be alive. I stood in wonder, savoring to the full the sights, the smells, the sounds. This was what I was looking for.

The street sign above my head said "Herald Square." So I stood at the corner at 34th and Broadway, in the city of New York, and discovered America.

"This is life!" I said out loud. "This is for me!"

I walked with the crowds . . . where I stood again and marveled at the hundreds of great electric signs, the many movie houses, the orange-juice stands, and the hawkers on the sidewalks. I stopped at one of the stands and had a hot dog. It was good, and I had another, with a glass of thin, orange-flavored liquid. I walked and walked, loving every sight, every sound, every smell. . ..

So long as I live I will never forget that moment. For it was then that I knew my destiny and knew that all my long years of hoping and planning were right, and meant to be. I knew that dreams could come true. In one of those flashes of knowing, I saw that my life would be here, in this great rushing roaring city full of the sights and sounds and smells of life.

I knew that I would not go back to France, not now. Not until I had made my success, and that I was sure would come, too.

Salom Rizk
American born in Syria

Another immigrant's words recorded in the same book are those of Salom Rizk. Salom was an orphan in Syria just after World War I. He learned that his father had been a United States citizen, and decided he would come here. In 1924, he was finally able to come to Ames, Iowa. He wanted to become truly American, and go to college in Ames. He started by going to public high school and working as a dishwasher in a Greek restaurant to make money. One day someone came into the restaurant and invited him to speak in front of a group of international businessmen to tell what it was like to become "Americanized." Salom was very nervous, and practiced many hours for his big speech.

Salom was later sent by Readers' Digest to 1,500 schools to talk about his experiences. He called his speeches "The Americanization of an American" and later wrote a book called Syrian Yankee.

I knew I was next. My heart was racing like a windmill. When Dr. Helser said, "I'm happy to

FOLD

present Sam Rizk, an American who had to dis-cover his own country." I struggled to my feet.

For a moment that seemed endless my memory was a complete emptiness. Then I remembered what I wanted to say.

"Ladies and gentlemen," I started, and I was suddenly terrified by the thickness of my accent. "Please do not think that I am a speaker. I am not a speaker. I am only a dishwater. I mean, I am only a dishwasher."

Well, everybody laughed so hard I began to wonder if they were ever going to stop. But after that everything became easy. The friendliest thing in the world is a laugh, even when it is at your own expense. I forgot my prepared speech and told my story just the way I had told it to the kids at school: how I was born in Syria and my mother died, leaving me to be cared for by a grandmother. How the death of my grandmother left me a miserable and ragged orphan in war-torn Syria. How I managed to survive by eating raw birds' eggs and roots in the hills. How I learned I was an American citizen. How it took five long, painful years to prove it. How at last I came to America, and how I felt when I saw this vast, rich land with its great farms and teeming

cities. How I appreciated the privileges of this miraculous land, the friendliness of the people, especially those who had helped me so much in Ames.

When I got through, I sat down, and everybody else stood up. They applauded and applauded until Mr. Davis motioned me to stand up, too. I knew they were not applauding me. They were applauding America, the land where something like this could happen to anybody, a land where a man was free, with the help of his fellows, to work out his own destiny. I knew that I was living proof to them of what America was and what America could be. They were proud of a nation because of me. But I could not feel proud. It was a very great and a humbling experience. When the meeting broke up, everybody came to shake hands with me. People invited me to their homes. They offered to lend me money to fulfill my ambitions. This sudden flood of warmth and generosity awakened in me a feeling I had been trying to capture from the first day I landed. For the first time I really felt that I was an American, that I belonged to these people and they belonged to me.

Name _____

When I First Came To This Land

In 1948, the folk singer, Oscar Brand, wrote this song about the challenges immigrants faced coming to this country.

1.

When I first came to this land.
I was not a wealthy man.
Then I built myself a shack.
I did what I could.
I called my shack, *Break-my-back*.
But the land was sweet and good;
I did what I could.

2.

When I first came to this land.
I was not a wealthy man.
Then I bought myself a cow.
I did what I could.
I called my cow, *No-milk-now*,
But the land was sweet and good;
I did what I could.

3.

When I first came to this land.
I was not a wealthy man.
Then I bought myself a duck.
I did what I could.
I called my duck, *Out-of-luck*,
But the land was sweet and good;
I did what I could.

4.

When I first came to this land.
I was not a wealthy man.
Then I got myself a wife.
I did what I could.
I called my wife, *Run-for-your-life*,
But the land was sweet and good;
I did what I could.

5.

When I first came to this land.
I was not a wealthy man.
Then I got myself a son.
I did what I could.
I called my son, *My-work's-done*
But the land was sweet and good;
I did what I could.

Name _____

Famous Immigrants

What do Albert Einstein, Alexander Graham Bell, Bob Hope, and Martina Navratilova have in common? They were all immigrants to the United States. All immigrants contribute to American culture after they arrive. Many immigrants have changed the course of our history. Here is a chart of some well-known Americans—who happen to have been immigrants. Use the blanks at the end to fill in information about some immigrants you know of who have made important contributions. They might even be your relatives!

IMMIGRANT	DATES	COUNTRY OF ORIGIN	CONTRIBUTION
Mary Antin*	1881-1949	Russia	Writer
Isaac Asimov*	1920-1992	Russia	Writer
Charles Atlas*	1893-1972	Italy	Bodybuilder
John J. Audubon	1785-1851	French West Indies	Ornithologist
Mikhail Baryshnikov	1948-	Latvia	Ballet Dancer
Abraham Beame*	1906-	England	Politician
Alexander G. Bell	1847-1922	Scotland	Inventor
Irving Berlin*	1888-1989	Russia	Composer
Elizabeth Blackwell	1821-1910	England	Doctor
Frank Capra*	1897-1991	Italy	Director
Andrew Carnegie	1837-1919	Scotland	Industrialist
Claudette Colbert*	1903-1996	France	Actor
Edward Corsi*	1896-1965	Italy	Politician
Albert Einstein	1879-1955	Germany	Physicist
Enrico Fermi	1901-1954	Italy	Physicist
Felix Frankfurter*	1882-1965	Austria	Supreme Court Justice
Greta Garbo*	1905-1996	Sweden	Actor
Marcus Garvey*	1887-1940	Jamaica	Activist
Emma Goldman*	1869-1940	Russia	Political Activist
Samuel Goldwyn*	1882-1974	Poland	Producer
Alexander Hamilton	1755-1804	British West Indies	Statesman
Joe Hill*	1879-1915	Sweden	Activist

IMMIGRANT	DATES	COUNTRY OF ORIGIN	CONTRIBUTION
Sidney Hillman*	1887-1946	Lithuania	Union Leader
Bob Hope*	1903-	England	Comedian
Al Jolson*	1886-1950	Lithuania	Jazz Singer
John Paul Jones	1747-1792	Scotland	Naval Officer
Elia Kazan*	1909-	Turkey	Director
Bela Lugosi*	1882-1956	Hungary	Actor
John Muir	1838-1914	Scotland	Naturalist
Martina Navratilova	1956-	Czechoslovakia	Tennis Player
Akeem Olajawon	1963-	Nigeria	Basketball Player
Mary Pickford	1893-1979	Canada	Actor
Frank Puglia*	1892-1975	Italy	Actor
Joseph Pulitzer	1847-1911	Hungary	Journalist
James Reston*	1909-1995	Scotland	Journalist
Knute Rockne*	1888-1931	Norway	Football Coach
Levi Strauss	1829-1902	Germany	Entrepreneur
Baron von Trapp*	1881-1948	Austria	Singer
Rudolph Valentino*	1895-1926	Italy	Actor

_____ _____ _____ _____

_____ _____ _____ _____

_____ _____ _____ _____

_____ _____ _____ _____

_____ _____ _____ _____

* These people immigrated through Ellis Island off New York City.

THE CULTURAL MOSAIC:
IMMIGRATION TODAY

If you read the papers and listen to news reports and politicians, you might get the idea that we are in the midst of an unprecedented immigration explosion. Now that your students have a background in the history of immigration in our country, they are equipped to look at actual figures to determine whether or not this impression is accurate.

In fact, the numbers are not history-setting. However, the demographics are different. During the great wave of immigration in the early 1900s, most immigrants came from western Europe. Today, most immigrants come from Hispanic and Asian countries.

The beginning of this unit, "Who We Are" will take a look at these and other population figures from the latest census breakdowns. Students will participate in analyzing the data and will be invited to make their own charts and graphs. As part of "Who We Are," students will take an in-depth look at their own roots, through oral history and family-tree activities.

F•Y•I

In the mid-1700s, it took 15 weeks to cross the Atlantic. In the mid-1800s, it took 15 days. Today, it takes roughly 6 hours on a jet plane.

The unit then looks beyond the figures to the realities of life for immigrants and non-immigrants today. Newcomers face many of the same issues that students explored in the last unit. Citizens already here are also grappling with some of the same, and some new issues. This unit will help you introduce your students to some of the economic and legal controversies in our country today. These issues require extra sensitivity on your part. The **Talking Points** are optional opportunities for you to engage your students in debates on these topics.

The **Literature Links** describe well-written books that will help students hear the voices of many immigrants describing how they feel about living in America.

WHO WE ARE

The following activities will help students gain an understanding of their own family histories and help them to understand who the American people are by analyzing data.

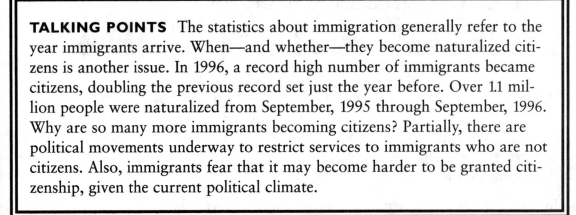

Our Population

ACTIVITY Share the graphs and charts on page 57 and 58 with your students. You may want to explain how to read the different kinds of graphs shown. Have students make up questions for each other based on the graphs, such as: Did more immigrants come from Asia or Europe between 1820 and 1993?

Our Roots: Family Trees and Oral Histories

ACTIVITY We can all find out more about who we are as a nation by investigating who we are individually. Help students conduct their own oral histories of people in their families or communities. Use the oral history reproducible on page 61 to get students started with some basic interview questions. You can also encourage your students to do their own family trees. The model provided on page 60 allows students with all different types of families to complete the tree without feeling excluded. Students can use spaces for step-parents, uncles, aunts, godparents, or other important family members. Encourage flexible use of this construction, to foster an understanding of the variety of family structures. (There may be certain family issues, such as adoption, which would make this a difficult activity for some students. Skip these activities if you have such concerns.)

A good way to begin is to use the Family Tree Know-Want-Learn reproducible on page 59. After they have completed their Family Tree they can return to their K-W-L chart and fill in "What I Still Want to Learn."

Our Community History Celebration

After students have completed their family trees and oral histories, plan an "Our Community History" celebration. Set up reports, family trees, and cassettes for your students' family and friends to share the information gathered by your junior historians. Share these tips on conducting an interview before distributing the oral history reproducible on page 61.

TIPS FOR DOING AN INTERVIEW

- Find out some basic background information about the person, if possible. It might help you think of ideas.

- Write a list of questions. Keep in mind the reporters' basics: Who, What, When, Where, and Why.

- Pick a quiet spot that's convenient for your interviewee. Make sure you allot plenty of time. Be prompt, and be respectful.

- Check out your tape recording equipment and tape. Make sure you have plenty of tapes and batteries, if needed. Even if you're taping, take notes.

- Be a good listener! Make sure they have enough time to answer, and whatever you do—DON'T INTERRUPT.

- Ask open-ended questions, and let people stretch out into their own stories.

Some sample questions: What did your grandparents tell you about their lives? What did you do for fun when you were my age? How has this town changed?

Further Reading: *Know Your Hometown History*, by Abigail Jungreis
New York: Franklin Watts, 1992.

My Backyard History Book by David Weitzman
Boston: Little Brown and Company, 1975.

CELEBRATING DIVERSITY

You've heard all the metaphors to describe our population: melting pot, crazy quilt, mosaic, tossed salad, rainbow—and probably more. Solicit these terms from your students. Then ask them to consider what the different terms imply about our population. Some connote a blending of cultures, while others suggest maintenance of national identities. Which do your students think are the most appropriate terms? Can they think of any others?

Class Quilt

During this activity, you might want to read the following quote aloud:

> America is not like a blanket—one piece of unbroken cloth, the same color, the same texture, the same size. America is more like a quilt—many pieces, many colors, many sizes, all woven together by a common thread.
>
> — Jesse Jackson, 20th century political leader

Distribute 8-inch square pieces of construction paper to each of your students. Ask them to decorate their panels with anything they can think of representing the culture of their families. Encourage the use of diverse materials and themes. Students might use fabric, photographs, magazines, food packaging or recipes, copies of documents, essays, or small objects collected from home. They can reinforce their squares with cardboard, if necessary.

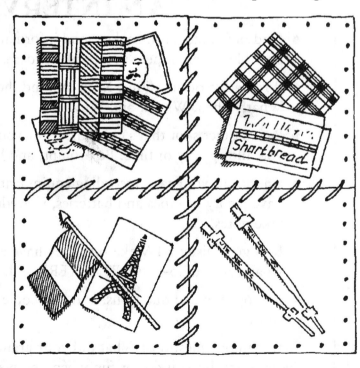

When they have completed their squares, have them punch holes around the edges with a hole-punch. Take colorful yarn, and show students how to lace their quilt together. Make sure to display the finished quilt!

Cultural Mosaic

During this activity, you may want to read the following quote aloud:

> We become not a melting pot but a beautiful mosaic. Different people, different beliefs, different yearnings, different hopes, different dreams.
> — former President Jimmy Carter

Distribute simple outline figures of people. Have students leaf through magazines cutting out pictures of people. They can rip out pieces showing different skin colors, and glue them onto their outline figures in a mosaic pattern. The completed projects should reflect all possible gradations of skin color. Make sure the magazines provided represent different cultures.

The American Rainbow

Distribute the reproducible on page 62. Students can color the different arcs representing food, homes, religions, families, customs, languages, and recreation with the different colors of the rainbow. Then have them fill in the bands with words related to their own cultures.

TALKING POINTS When groups of immigrants come to our country, they frequently settle in neighborhoods centered around their homelands. Enclaves exist in these neighborhoods, with customs, businesses, and foods like those found in the "old country." Conversely, many immigrants assimilate rapidly and thoroughly into United States culture—forgoing their traditional holidays, and language, and adopting American ways. Which method of adaptation do students think is preferable? Is some balance between the two possible?

AUDIOTAPE Students can hear the voices of immigrants who are recent arrivals to America on the audiotape.

WELCOMING NEWCOMERS

Ask students if they have ever moved. Even if they haven't come here from another country, they may have moved to a new town or neighborhood. How did they feel? Were they nervous to start at a new school? Shy to sit down at a lunch table in the cafeteria? Lonely? Solicit their memories of relocation. Then ask them to imagine that they also didn't speak the language or know the customs of the country.

F•Y•I

Population on the Move: 42 million Americans moved during a recent one-year period—mostly within our own country.

You're Always Welcome

Ask students if anyone helped them when they moved. Have your students work in groups to prepare "Welcome Kits to Newcomers"—either Americans or foreign immigrants—to your town.

Their kits can include recipe books, local maps, listings of special community events, and resource lists. They should also make a brochure (see below).

Help them contact your local Chamber of Commerce for ideas.

ACTIVITY

"Welcome to Our Town" Brochure

Help students use the reproducible on page 63 to make a "Welcome to Our Town" brochure. The reproducible shows them how this origami book folds up. Then they can use a fresh 8 1/2 by 11-inch sheet of paper (or larger) to make their brochures.

LITERATURE LINK

Hello, My Name is Scrambled Eggs
by Jamie Gilson
New York: Lothrop, Lee & Shepard, 1985.

The Story: This amusing story describes what happens when a well-meaning boy named Harvey tries to help a newly-arrived Vietnamese boy, Nguyen, learn about his new country. He begins by labeling everything with "Hello, My Name is. . ." tags to help Nguyen learn English. In the process, both boys learn about cultural identity, and about friendship.

LITERATURE ACTIVITY

Making Name Tags

Buy or make some "Hello, My Name Is. . ." tags. Choose a language other than English. You might choose Spanish, especially if your class has a large Hispanic population. Provide a foreign language dictionary for that language. Ask students to label things around the classroom in an effort to learn the names. Use this activity to discuss what happens when Harvey tries to teach Nguyen English. Discuss the conflict between assimilation and maintaining cultural identity.

You can also use the same tags to write "hello" in different languages. Have the students wear their name tags around for a week. Each child can then practice saying hello to other students in the languages on their tags.

> # HELLO
> MY NAME IS

I'm New Here
by Bud Howlett
Boston: Houghton Mifflin Company, 1993.

Background Information: The author, Bud Howlett, was a teacher and elementary school principal in California for over 25 years. Now he is a full-time writer and photographer, and has put both skills to work in this book on cultural adaptation. His concerns about bilingual education and his general sympathy for children combine to make a very affecting portrait of a girl's first days in this country. The touching story is told from Jazmin's point of view.

The Story: Jazmin Escalante has just moved to the United States from El Salvador. She speaks no English, and is frightened to start her first day in fifth grade. She has a terrible first day, when she gets put a grade behind with a teacher and students who speak no Spanish. From there, she makes small but meaningful steps toward fitting in and toward learning. She makes the winning goal in a soccer game. Even better, she makes a friend who teaches her some English and holds her hand. At that point, she says, "I didn't feel like I was new here anymore."

LITERATURE ACTIVITY

First Days
Even if students are not immigrants, they have probably had a first day somewhere. They may have moved to a new town, started a new school, or joined a team late in the year. At some point, they have probably had the experience of feeling like the new kid. Invite them to write stories about what their first days were like. Did anything happen that made them feel more comfortable? You can use the directions on page 63 to make a picture book for their stories. If there are any children in your class who are new, encourage the other students to think of ways they can help make the adjustment easier.

LITERATURE LINK

Over Here It's Different: Carolina's Story
by Mildred Leinweber Dawson
New York: Macmillan Publishing Company, 1993.

Background Information: There is a large and growing Dominican population in our country. Carolina Liranzo was born in the Dominican Republic and moved to the United States when she was seven. She is 11 now, and lives in a community in Queens, New York, with many other immigrants from the Caribbean. She has an extended family who has gradually come over "one by

one." They have helped each other out with the difficult transition. This is a nonfiction account of Carolina's life and how she feels about her two countries. She misses her old home and her grandfather, and is trying to retain some aspects of Dominican culture. Her old life was in many ways quieter and less stressful. But she appreciates all of the opportunities she has and her new friends.

Mildred Leinweber Dawson is a former Foreign Service officer. She gives a good sense of some of the processes necessary for Carolina and her relatives to immigrate. There is an unusual amount of accurate information worked into the text about the history of immigration, life in the Dominican Republic, and other social-studies rich topics.

What If?

LITERATURE ACTIVITY

When Carolina lived in the Dominican Republic, her grandparents did not have much electricity. She couldn't watch television or videos, the way she sees kids in Queens, New York, spending some of their after school hours. Ask your students to spend one or two days after school using no electricity. How does it change their activities? Can they still have fun?

Let's Cook

LITERATURE ACTIVITY

One thing Carolina misses about her old home is the food. They travel to other neighborhoods to buy special ingredients. Here is a treat from the Caribbean that your students can make easily:

COCONUT PINEAPPLE BALLS
Ingredients
1 1/2 cups dried, uncooked pineapple (6 ounces)
2 cups shredded coconut
2/3 cup sweetened condensed milk
1 cup confectioners' sugar
Directions
1. Chop pineapples into small pieces, or grind them in a blender.
2. Add coconut.
3. Stir in condensed milk.
4. Pour 1 cup confectioners' sugar into a separate bowl.
5. Shape pineapple mixture into balls.
6. Roll balls in sugar one at a time.

CHALLENGES

ECONOMIC ISSUES

Immigrants generally come to this country full of ambition to work hard and improve their lives. They start new businesses, create jobs, and contribute to their communities in many ways. In the eyes of some, however, these newcomers use vital resources and services, and take from a limited pool of jobs.

Myths and Realities

Use the information that follows to help clarify some of the myths and realities about the impact of immigration on today's economy.

On Welfare
Of immigrants who entered the United States in the 1980s (excluding refugees), 2 percent live on welfare while 3.7 percent of working-age, native-born Americans receive welfare. In one state studied, Illinois, non-immigrant households were 40 percent more likely to receive welfare than immigrants.

On Public Services
Immigrants pay $25 billion in taxes, far more than they use in government services.

On Income and Spending
Immigrant spending equals about 8 percent of total national spending. That's the same amount as the percentage of immigrants in the general population.

On Jobs
Immigrants are self-employed at higher rates than non-immigrants. Immigrants create more jobs than they fill.

Immigration on the Rise

New Study Shows Decline in Immigration

Use this opportunity to discuss the meaning of statistics generally with your class. Point out that people can manipulate statistics to advance their agendas. Statistics do lend credibility to arguments. Find examples in current newspapers and magazines, and ask students to look beyond the statistics to the points they support. Have students find examples of different people using the same data to draw different conclusions.

TALKING POINTS Some people say that immigrants fuel the economy, with their willingness to work long hours for lower wages. Others say that they take jobs away from native-born citizens. Do immigrants enlarge the pie—or take a slice from the total economy?

DISCRIMINATION

LITERATURE LINK

In the Year of the Boar and Jackie Robinson
by Bette Bao Lord
New York: Harper & Row, 1984.

Background Information: Although the story is fiction, the author, Bette Bao Lord, was an immigrant from China. She was born in Shanghai in 1938 and moved to Brooklyn when she was eight years old. She faced many of the same difficulties that Shirley Temple Wong faces in this novel. Although the story takes place in 1947, it is very relevant to teaching about the problems of discrimination faced by students today. The pen-and-ink drawings combine Chinese and American cultures. The story is action-packed, funny, and touching—and makes for a good, fast read-aloud.

The Story: Known as Sixth Cousin in China, an immigrant girl gives herself a new name to greet her new world, in Brooklyn, New York. Shirley Temple Wong struggles with English, and the new culture. She overcomes her difficulties and connects with her peers through her love for America's pastime: baseball. She shares much in common with her hero, Jackie Robinson, as she battles against discrimination.

LITERATURE ACTIVITY

I Pledge...:
Read Shirley's version of "I Pledge Allegiance":
I pledge a lesson to the frog of the United States of America, and to the wee puppet for witches' hands. One Asian, in the vestibule, with little tea and just rice for all." Have students ever misunderstood song lyrics, speeches, or anything else? Encourage them to share such anecdotes. Then write the real text of the pledge on the chalkboard. Ask students to translate the words into simple language that someone who spoke another language might better understand.

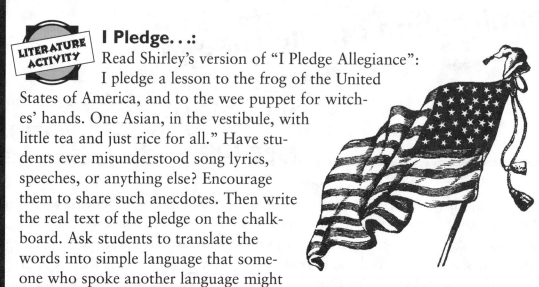

What's Your Sign?

1947 is the year of the Boar, 4646. Explain to your students a little bit about the Chinese astrological calendar. Each year is assigned an animal's name, which is repeated every 12 years. Use this calendar to help students identify the animal for the year they were born, and the animal for the current year.

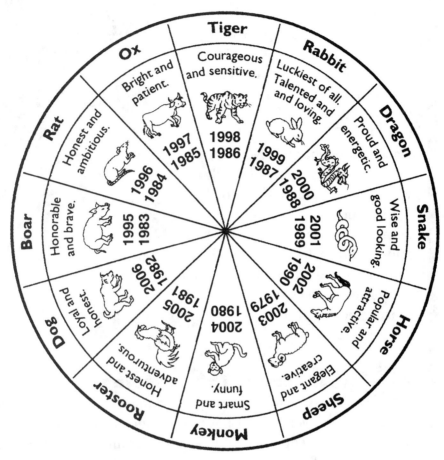

LITERATURE LINK

Molly's Pilgrim

by Barbara Cohen
New York: Lothrop, Lee & Shepard, 1983.

Background Information: This book by Barbara Cohen is listed as a notable children's trade book in the field of social studies, and has won an IRA/CBC Children's Choice award. It was made into a movie which won the 1986 Academy Award for Live Short Film. The author said she was able to write her book because, "I knew about being on the outside and hungering to get in." She died in 1992 but some of her 30 books for children have continued to be published posthumously. This book is suitable for younger children, but could work as a read-aloud for older students as well.

The Story: Molly is a Jewish immigrant from Russia. She faces discrimination by her classmates, who make fun of her looks, her clothes, and her speech. She is the only Jewish student in her school, and wants desperately to return to Russia or go to New York City.

When Molly's teacher gives a homework assignment to study Thanksgiving and make a Pilgrim doll, Molly learns a valuable lesson. Her mother lets her know that "it takes all kinds of pilgrims to make a Thanksgiving." Her teacher adds that Molly's family members are "modern day Pilgrims who came to America to worship God in their own way, in peace and freedom." Over the course of the story, Molly and her classmates come to better understand each other. Their teacher explains that the custom of Thanksgiving actually comes from a Jewish holiday (Sukkos). In the process, Molly makes a good friend. The story builds an appreciation for different cultures. Perhaps more importantly, it is likely to inspire compassion and empathy in readers of any culture.

LITERATURE ACTIVITY

All About Thanksgiving

Have students research Thanksgiving. What are some of the different versions of how the holiday originated? What are some of the different ways people celebrate it in our country? In your classroom? Are there any versions of Thanksgiving in other countries? Have students present their reports to the class. Compare and contrast the different theories. Make sure students state where they got their information.

LITERATURE LINK

I Speak English for My Mom

by Muriel Staneck.
Morton Grove, Illinois: Albert Whitman & Company, 1989.

Background Information: Children frequently pick up a new language more quickly than adults. This is partially because children's brains are more receptive to different sounds. But with immigrants, there are other reasons as well. Children may be less afraid to learn, have more desire to assimilate, and have more exposure through school and friends. This difference can sometimes turn the parent/child relationship on its head. If any of your students are in this position, invite them to share their experiences with the class.

The Story: Lupe is a Mexican-American girl who speaks better English than her mother, Mrs. Gomez. "When I was small," she says, "Mom helped me do everything. Now that I'm older, I have to help my mom because I can speak English, and she can't." Lupe speaks English at school, but Spanish at home with her mother. At first, Lupe seems to be having fun. She enjoys helping and even plays jokes on her mom, teasing her that the doctor prescribed ice cream. But during the course of the story, her mother's lack of fluency creates problems for the family. It takes Lupe away from her friends, and creates financial problems when Mrs. Gomez loses her sewing job. The story comes to a positive conclusion when her mother decides to take English classes, and Lupe helps her with her homework.

Role Reversals

Have your students ever experienced a time when they took care of a parent, or helped them in a grown-up way? How did it make them feel? How did it make their parents feel? Have them work in groups to create dramas reenacting these events.

TALKING POINTS In *I Speak English for My Mom*, a girl tries to translate and help her mother function in her community. One controversial issue in the public forum today is whether English should be declared the official language. English is spoken in the vast majority of homes, and is used in government, business, and schools. But many citizens speak predominantly Spanish. What would the proposed law do? Help your students to research both sides of the issue. How many languages are spoken by the children in your school?

REFUGEES

One Day We Had to Run

by Sybella Wilkes

Brookfield, CT: The Millbrook Press, 1994.

Background Information: This book tells the stories of three children who were African refugees. They had made their way to refugee camps in Kenya, where they met Sybella Wilkes, the editor/author of this collection. The children were so traumatized by the death, poverty, and despair of their homelands that they could not tell their stories at first. Wilkes got them to paint and tell folktales as a way to break through their silence. This book gives detailed information about the history, demographics, and politics of the three countries: Sudan, Somalia, and Ethiopia. The children's artwork, folktales, and personal stories are collected in a powerful presentation of the effects of poverty and war on children. Your students will surely be moved, and some may be prompted to volunteer for Save the Children and other organizations mentioned in the book.

Teaching Tip

A **refugee** is defined in the book as "someone who has fled across a national border from his or her home country, or is unable to return to it, because of a well-founded fear that he or she will be persecuted for reasons of race, religion, nationality, or political opinion. Refugees who cross borders because of famine are not necessarily covered by international protection, unlike refugees fleeing from war."

A **displaced person** is defined as "someone who has been forced to move to another part of his or her own country because of war, famine, or disaster."

F•Y•I

There are more than 20 million refugees in the world today. Eighty percent are women and children.

LITERATURE ACTIVITY

Making Pictures

Show students some of the pictures in the book first and see if they can determine what is being expressed. Then read the stories. Ask students to create pictures of something important that happened in their lives. Share the pictures among the class, and then invite students to relate their actual stories. Encourage students to choose topics that deal with some of the feelings of being displaced, if they have any such experiences.

LITERATURE LINK

How Many Days to America? A Thanksgiving Story
by Eve Bunting
Boston: Houghton Mifflin, 1988.

Background Information: This book does not specify when the story is taking place or from where the main characters are fleeing. That ambiguity may be part of what lends the tale a universal quality. The main event—a boat ride to freedom—sums up all of immigration in one powerfully described journey. The sleuth can determine, however, that the tale is contemporary, and the family is probably from Jamaica. Thanksgiving is thrown into the mix for good measure, but is really not necessary to carry the book's message. The picture book presentation allows easy access for young readers, but the content would be appropriate for older students as well. The repeated refrains make this a good read-aloud choice.

The Story: The family in this picture book leaves its homeland because it feels threatened by the government and the military. As the father explains to his son, they leave "because we do not think the way they think." They leave all their belongings behind and board a crowded boat in the dead of night. Their journey is described in detail. They arrive safely, by coincidence on Thanksgiving Day. They are welcomed and share in a feast. A woman explains the custom to them: "Long ago, unhappy people came here to start new lives," the woman said. "They celebrated by giving thanks. The father adds, "that is the only true way to celebrate."

LITERATURE ACTIVITY

Preparing a Feast

Plan a feast with your class. Everyone can bring something that is a specialty from his or her home. During the meal, go around the table. Each student should pretend he is talking to the family in this book. How would they explain Thanksgiving? How would they explain the food and the customs?

LIFE IN A NEW LAND

One outgrowth of the history of immigration is the formation of enclaves of immigrant groups in specific neighborhoods. Through relatives and word of mouth, immigrants from the same country often form their own communities and gather in pockets within larger cities. There they find support and can maintain some of their culture. They can find specialty food items. They can also help each other find work.

There are several series of nonfiction books available that cover specific immigrant communities. If your students are particularly interested in one group, these series offer a good introduction.

LITERATURE LINK

Cultures of America
series by Marshall Cavendish Corporation
North Bellmore, New York, 1995.

Description: Books in this series include Jewish Americans, African Americans, French Americans, Greek Americans, and Cuban Americans. They follow a similar format, covering *Leaving a Homeland, Life in a New Land, Family and Community, Religion and Celebrations, Customs, Expressions and*

Hospitality, and *Contributions to American Culture*. The text is very thorough and gives a strong sense of the different cultures. The series, however, suffers from a lack of individual voices, and is told primarily in an expository way.

A World of My Own

Series by Lodestar Books
New York: Dutton

Description: All the books in this series so far are written by Kathy Krull with photographs by David Hautzig. The series examines children living in specific communities, covering one place in depth per book. Books include:

One Nation, Many Tribes: How Kids Live in Milwaukee's Indian Community
Bridges to Change: How Kids Live on a South Carolina Sea Island
The Other Side: How Kids Live in a California Latino Neighborhood
City Within a City: How Kids Live in New York's Chinatown

These books not only give a detailed look at the communities, with specific people quoted and photographed, but they also provide a strong sense of the cultures. They treat the interplay between the larger communities and these enclaves. They do not hesitate to deal with stereotypes and economic issues.

American Voices

series by Rourke Corporation
Vero Beach, Florida, 1991

Description: Similar to the *Cultures of America* series, these books all follow the same format: they give an overview of the nationality in North America and talk about the culture of the immigrant community. They then cover why immigrants came, when they arrived, where they went, and what they do. Two final chapters cover contributions and famous immigrants from the country involved. These books are jam-packed with information, some of which connotes flavor and some of which is dry and statistical. Time lines, glossaries, resources, and bibliographies in the back of the book could be very useful. As with *Cultures of America*, there are few quotes or photographs showing real people, today.

LITERATURE ACTIVITY

Americanization Poster

In all of the books in the three series described above, an underlying theme is the conflict between assimilating and maintaining one's cultural identity. Reproduce the poster on page 64, advertising a school for Americanization in 1920. The goal was to teach English and citizenship to immigrants. Point out to students that the Immigration and Naturalization Service (INS) provides adult immigrants with educational material about the United States. State and local governments make further efforts in helping immigrants adjust and adapt. Encourage students to create their own posters directed at new immigrants.

Name _____

Our Population

The graphs below and on the next page tell about our country's population and immigration history. Are there any statistics that surprise you? Use the graphs to make up questions to ask your classmates.

DEMOGRAPHICS - THE CHANGING FACE OF THE NATION

Population distribution of the U.S. by race and ethnic origin; whites and blacks include only those who did not identify themselves as being of Hispanic origin. Numbers do not add up to 100 because of rounding, and because American Indians are not shown. Source: Census Bureau

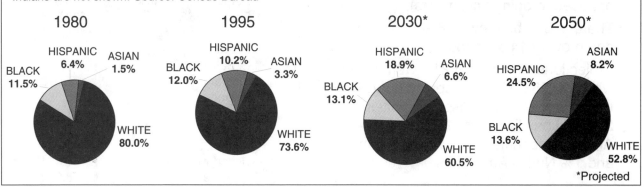

1980
HISPANIC 6.4%
ASIAN 1.5%
BLACK 11.5%
WHITE 80.0%

1995
HISPANIC 10.2%
ASIAN 3.3%
BLACK 12.0%
WHITE 73.6%

2030*
HISPANIC 18.9%
ASIAN 6.6%
BLACK 13.1%
WHITE 60.5%

2050*
ASIAN 8.2%
HISPANIC 24.5%
BLACK 13.6%
WHITE 52.8%
*Projected

DID YOU KNOW?

- One quarter of the foreign-born population in our country today arrived in the last 5 years.
- One immigrant arrives every 35 seconds.
- One person is deported or leaves voluntarily every day.

Region of origin of immigrants to the United States, 1820-1993; source, U.S. Dept. of Justice, *1993, Statistical Yearbook of the Immigration and Naturalization Service (1994).*

Region	U.S. Total
Europe	37,566,702
North America	9,478,377
Asia	7,051,564
Caribbean	3,035,898
South America	1,440,413
Central America	1,046,963
Africa	417,926
Oceania	223,821
Unspecified	267,639
Other America	110,147

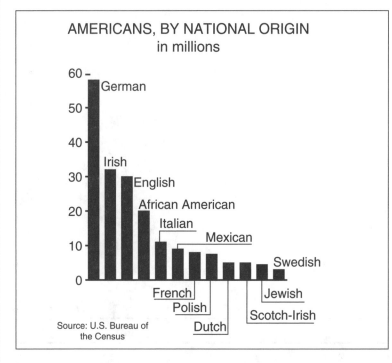

AMERICANS, BY NATIONAL ORIGIN
in millions

German, Irish, English, African American, Italian, French, Polish, Dutch, Mexican, Scotch-Irish, Jewish, Swedish

Source: U.S. Bureau of the Census

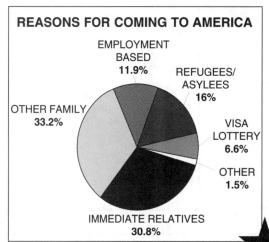

REASONS FOR COMING TO AMERICA

EMPLOYMENT BASED 11.9%
REFUGEES/ASYLEES 16%
OTHER FAMILY 33.2%
VISA LOTTERY 6.6%
OTHER 1.5%
IMMEDIATE RELATIVES 30.8%

Name _____

Our Population

DID YOU KNOW?

- U.S. adds one person to its population every 14 seconds—through birth and immigration. That's about 6,300 people every day. Two-thirds are born here (as opposed to being immigrants).

- There is one birth every 8 seconds, one death every 14 seconds.

- Projections: By the mid 21st Century, we will have 383 million people in our country. 53% will be non-Hispanic whites, 21% will be Hispanics, 15% will be African Americans, 10% will be Asians, and 1% Native Americans.

Country of last residence for immigrants to the U.S. 1991-93; source, U. S. Dept. of Justice, *1993, Statis-tical Yearbook of the Immigration and Naturalization Service (1994).*

Mexico	1,288,693
Philippines	195,634
Dominican Republic	128,834
Former USSR	128,834
India	116,201
China	111,324
El Salvador	99,794
Vietnam	77,913
Poland	68,885
Haiti	67,701
Canada	65,370
Korea	61,484
United Kingdom	59,114
Jamaica	58,018
Hong Kong	47,723

What is the distribution of ages found in your classroom, your grade, or your school? Conduct a survey, and make your own graph here. Be sure to give it a title!

y

x

Name _____

Family History K-W-L Chart

You probably know a little bit about your family history already. But there is probably even more that you don't know. Use the chart below to complete the two branches. Later, fill in the "roots." What have you learned about your roots?

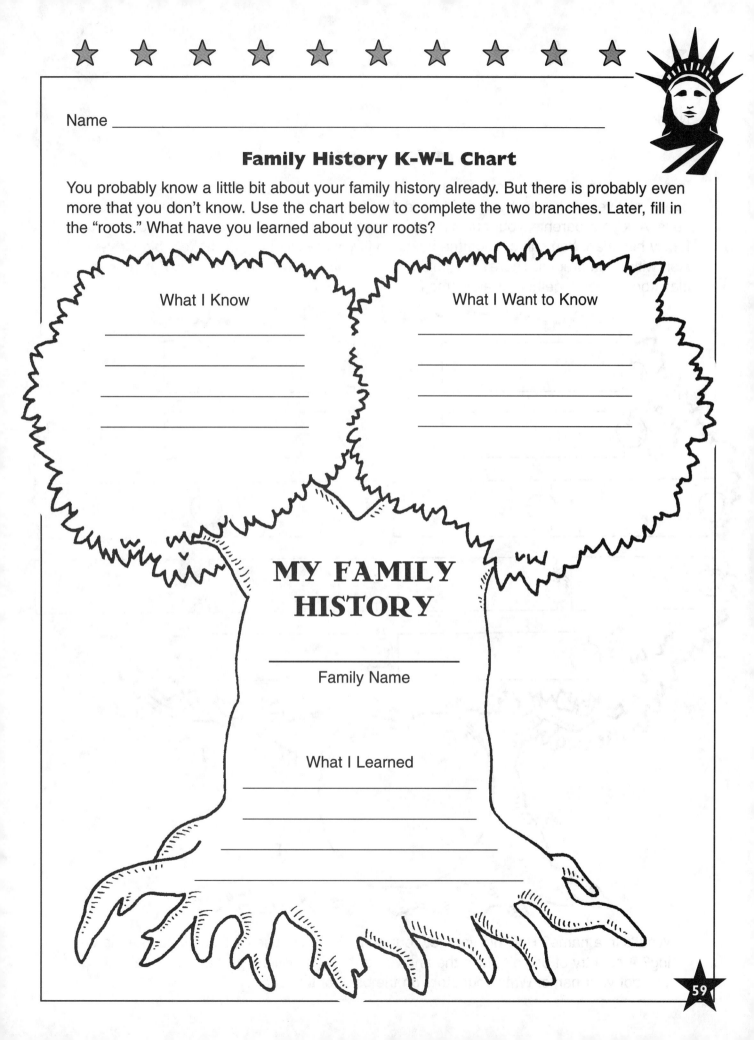

What I Know

_____
_____
_____
_____

What I Want to Know

_____
_____
_____
_____

MY FAMILY HISTORY

_____

Family Name

What I Learned

_____
_____
_____
_____

Name _____

My Family Tree

In each box on this family tree, fill in the whole name, date of birth, and birth place for every relative you know. If you don't have the information you need, start asking questions. Ask your parents, your aunts, uncles, grandparents. You're about to become your family historian. You can change the boxes to fit your family tree, or make a bigger version with photographs. There's no limit to how far back your tree can grow. Put your classroom trees together for a diverse forest.

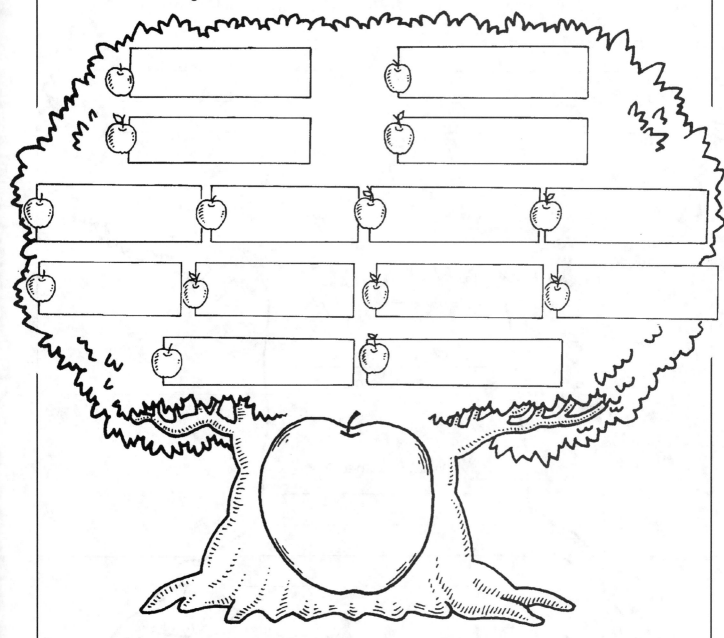

What's in a name? How did you get your name? Who chose it? Does it have a meaning? A country of origin? Make the answer to these questions part of a story about how you got your name. Write your story on the back of this page.

Name _____

Oral History

Conducted by _____

Name of Person _____ Age _____

Place of Birth _____

Question about childhood _____

Answer_____

_____

Question about places lived and why _____

Answer_____

Question about interests _____

Answer_____

_____

Most interesting story

_____

_____

_____

_____

Stop/Rewind/Play! Now write your notes up into a biography/oral history of your subject on the back of this page.

STOP/EJECT   REC   PLAY   REW   FF   PAUSE

Name _____

The American Rainbow

Fill in the bands with words and
colors showing the diversity
of our cultures.

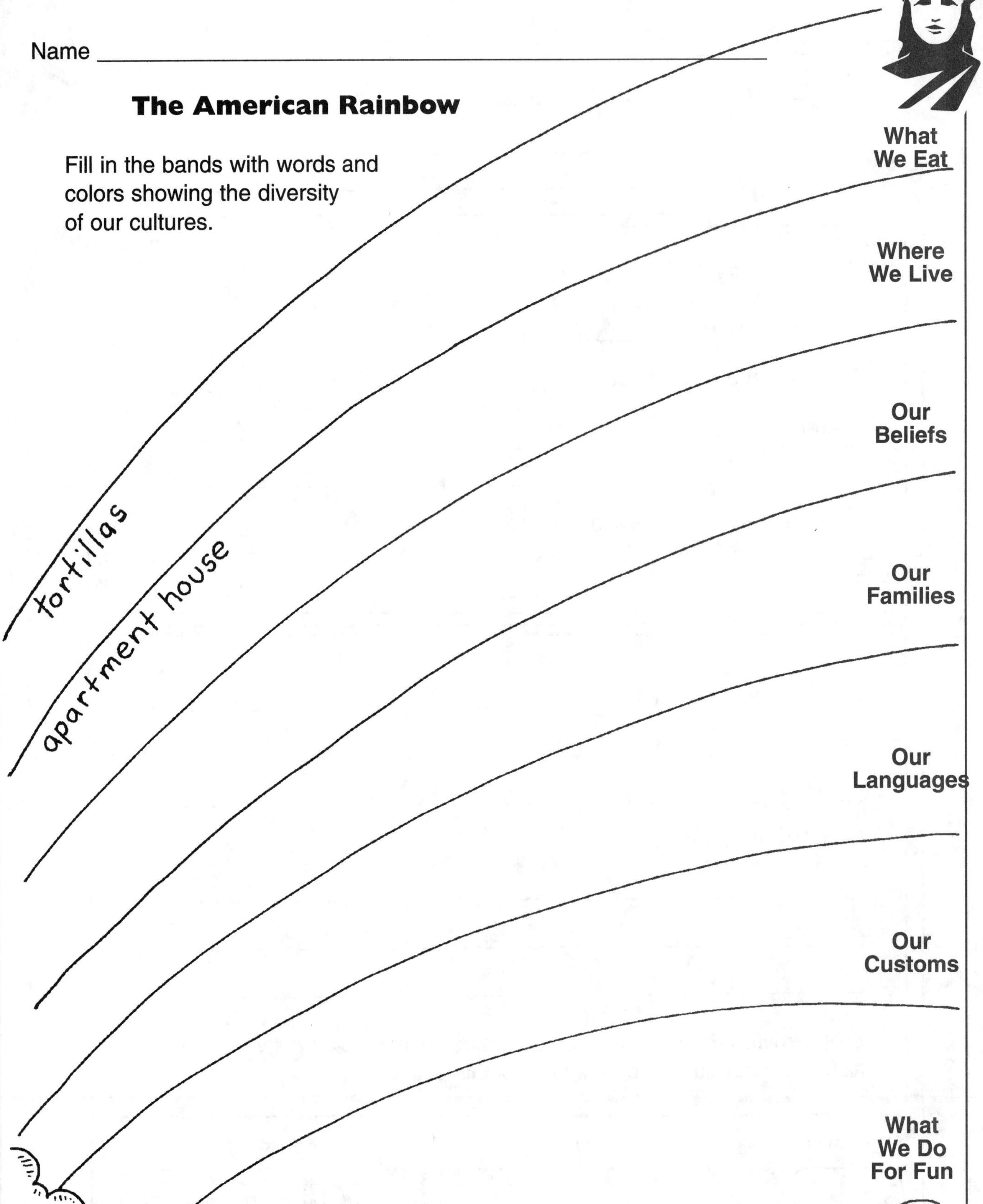

tortillas

apartment house

What
We Eat

Where
We Live

Our
Beliefs

Our
Families

Our
Languages

Our
Customs

What
We Do
For Fun

Welcome to Our Town

The diagrams below show you how to make a booklet from a single 8 1/2" x 11" sheet of paper. Follow the simple steps. Then create your own "Welcome To Our Town" brochure describing ways newcomers can enjoy your hometown.

 1.

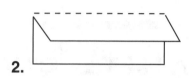 2.

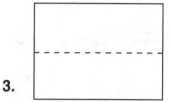 3.

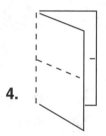 4.

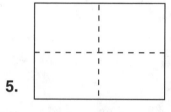 5.

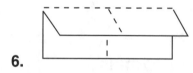 6.

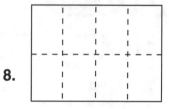 7.

8.

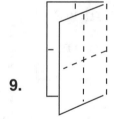 9.

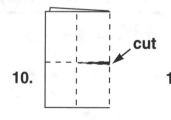 10.

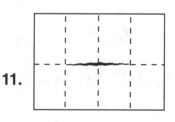 11.

 12. cut

13.

14.

15.

Name _____

Schools for Americanization

This poster was made in 1920. What does it tell you about people's view toward immigrants at that time? Create your own poster that would help immigrants make the adjustment to living in the United States today.

GRANITE CITY

AMERICANIZATION SCHOOLS

Monday
and
Thursday
Evenings
7:30 p. m.

Beginning
Monday,
September
the 27th,
1920

Underwood & Underwood

These two men are brothers, one is an American Citizen and the other has just come to this country with their old mother. See the difference in the way they dress and look. America is a great country. In America everybody has a chance. Everybody who comes to America from the old country ought to learn the American language and become an American citizen. If the people that come to America do not become Americans, this country will soon be like the old country.

SCHOOLS:

HIGH SCHOOL, 20TH AND D STREETS
LINCOLN PLACE, 917 PACIFIC AVENUE

LIBERTY SCHOOL, 20TH AND O STREETS
MADISON SCHOOL, 1322 MADISON AVENUE

Keep America Great.   Become an American Citizen   **Learn The Language.**

Press-Record Publishing Co. 1834 D St., Granite City, Ill

LIBERTY AND JUSTICE FOR ALL

ONE NATION

Americans, immigrants or not, all share many beliefs. In this unit, students explore the many aspects of citizenship that bring all Americans together.

LITERATURE LINK

I Hear America Singing
by Walt Whitman

Background Information: Share the two poems on this and the next page with your students. Let them know that both were written by famous American poets. Walt Whitman's poem is about the great diversity of the American people. He claimed to "hear America singing." Langston Hughes wrote "I, Too" ten years after the death of Whitman. While he appreciated Whitman's poetry, he felt that African-American voices such as his own were not being heard. Students can listen to the two poems on the audiotape.

AUDIOTAPE

I hear America singing, the varied carols I hear,
Those of mechanics, each one singing his as it should be blithe and strong,
The carpenter singing his as he measures his plank or beam,
The mason singing his as he makes ready for work, or leaves off work,
The boatman singing what belongs to him in his boat, the deck-hand singing on the
    steamboat deck.
The shoemaker singing as he sits on his bench, the hatter singing as he stands,
The wood-cutter's song, the ploughboy's on his way in the morning or at noon
    intermission or at sundown,
The delicious singing of the mother, or of the young wife at work, or of the girl
    sewing or washing,
Each singing what belongs to him or her and to none else,
The day what belongs to the day — at night the party of young fellows, robust,
    friendly,
Singing with open mouths their strong melodious songs.

I, TOO
by Langston Hughes

I, too, sing America.
I am the darker brother.
They send me to eat in the kitchen
When company comes,
But I laugh,
And eat well,
And grow strong.
Tomorrow,
I'll be at the table
When company comes.
Nobody'll dare
Say to me,
"Eat in the kitchen,"
Then.
Besides,
They'll see how beautiful I am
And be ashamed —
I, too, am America.

You, Too

Encourage your students to write poems that express their own, unique, American voices.

Our National Symbols

Many immigrants have strong feelings for the Statue of Liberty, the American flag, and other symbols of their new country. Point out to the students that all citizens can feel pride in their country. Use the reproducibles on pages 74-75 to remind students of some of our national symbols and encourage them to discuss their feelings about them.

CITIZENSHIP

THE PROCESS

Help students understand the process necessary to become a United States citizen. This process applies only to immigrants. However, "natural-born citizens"—people who are citizens by virtue of being born to United States citizens—share some of the same rights and responsibilities. Be sure that the discussion is broadened to include all citizens, not just immigrants.

Eligibility Requirements for Citizenship

- be at least 18 years old

- have lived in the United States as a legal resident for at least five years

- be of good moral character and loyal to the United States

- be able to read, write, and understand basic English

- have basic knowledge and understanding of the history, government, and the Constitution of the United States

- be willing to take the oath of allegiance to the United States

Encourage a discussion with your students about these requirements. What do they think is meant by "good moral character"?

ACTIVITY

Understanding the Oath

When immigrants come to the United States, they have many hurdles to cross before they can become citizens. They must fill out forms to see if they qualify. They get fingerprinted. They get interviewed and take tests. Many of them go through these stages knowing very little English, while adjusting to life in a new country. At the end of this process, new citizens take the "oath of allegiance" at a final court hearing. The oath was written over 200 years ago, and much of it is difficult to understand today. Read the oath below to your students.

I hereby declare, on oath, that I absolutely and entirely renounce and abjure all allegiance and fidelity to any foreign prince, potentate, state, or sovereignty of whom or which I have heretofore been a subject or citizen; that I will support and defend the Constitution and laws of the United States of America against all enemies, foreign and domestic; that I will bear true faith and allegiance to the same; that I will bear arms on behalf of the United States when required by the law, that I will perform noncombatant service in the Armed Forces of the United States when required by law; that I will perform work of national importance under civilian direction when required by the law; and that I take this obligation freely without any mental reservation of purpose of evasion, so help me God. In acknowledgment whereof I have hereunto affixed my signature.

Help your students to "translate" the language into words they know and use. You might write different parts of the oath on index cards and distribute them to small groups. Then ask students to write their own versions of the oath that would be easier for immigrants to understand.

- *There are some exceptions to the oath. Some people whose religious beliefs preclude military involvement are allowed to skip over that part of the oath.*

- *New citizens have the rights to vote, serve on juries, work for the government, travel freely, and help their relatives become citizens, too.*

ACTIVITY Citizenship Day

Citizenship Day is celebrated across the country every year on September 17th—the anniversary of the signing of the United States Constitution. Foreign-born people who have lived in the country for five years are eligible for citizenship. All over the country on this day, immigrants who meet the requirements for citizenship are sworn in. Help your students plan a Citizenship Day celebration (on the real holiday, or on any day you choose). You can use some of the other activities on these pages to make the holiday come to life.

ACTIVITY Making the Grade

Tell your students that all immigrants wishing to become United States citizens must pass a test showing their knowledge of the language, history, and government of our country. Give out the sample tests on pages 76 and 77 so that your students can test their own United States knowledge. They can work in small groups quizzing each other as if they were taking their oral examinations.

TALKING POINTS Immigrants who become citizens are called "naturalized citizens." They do not have the right to become President of the United States. How do your students feel about this restriction?

Further Reading: *I Pledge Allegiance*, by June Swanson.
Minneapolis: Carolrhoda Books, 1991.

IMMIGRATION LAWS

For about 100 years after we became a nation, our harbors offered free access to all who came. In 1882 the first law was passed excluding certain immigrants. Today, every session of Congress debates about immigration law. Who has priority for admission? Who should be excluded? How do we decide? What are the limits, if any?

Some of the key immigration laws, listed below, may help give your students an understanding of the progression of thinking about immigration in our country. Refer to the **poster** for other related information. You can work with your class to make an Immigration Law Time Line using this information.

IMMIGRATION LAWS

1882	Chinese Exclusion Act, preventing Chinese workers from entering the country
1882-1915	Laws written to exclude 33 categories of people, including political radicals and illiterates
1914	World War I arouses strong anti-immigrant feelings
1924	Quotas established for specific countries, including southern and eastern Europe
1960s	Fairness of quotas comes into question
1965	The Nationality Act raises the ceiling on quotas; allows equal access to all nationalities. Preference given to kin.
1980	Refugee Act grants access to refugees
1986	Reform Act forbids hiring of illegal immigrants; helps them become legal immigrants

Discuss current immigration laws with your students. They are complex, but the basic principles are as follows: no person can be refused immigration status because of race, nationality, or religion. Preference is given to relatives of citizens, to those with needed professional skills, to refugees from political and religious persecution, and to those from underrepresented countries.

F•Y•I

Relatives of naturalized citizens have surpassed refugees as the largest source of new immigrants.

TALKING POINTS Today, there are no quotas specific to countries of origin, but there are overall limits. Should there be restrictions on immigration? Why? Encourage your students to debate the issues. Have them pretend they are addressing a session of Congress to argue their points.

Who Belongs Here?

by Margery Burns Knight
Gardiner, ME: Tilbury House Publishers, 1993.

Background Information: Margery Burns Knight volunteered for the Peace Corps in Benin, Africa. She has taught English to recent immigrants. She and the illustrator, Anne Sibley O'Brien, worked together before to create the highly acclaimed *Talking Walls*. Although *Who Belongs Here?* is fictionalized, it is based on a true story and loaded with facts.

The Story: Nary was just a young boy when he escaped from Cambodia with his grandmother. Fleeing through the jungle, toward the Thai border, they left behind their friends and family. In America, Nary felt, "life would be better than heaven." When he arrives, the United States does offer freedom, safety, and comfort. But he also faces discrimination. He is told to "Get back on the boat and go home where you belong." The book then poses its central question, "What if Nary was forced to go back to Cambodia? What if everyone who now lives in the United States, but whose ancestors came from another country, was forced to return to his or her homeland?. . . Who would be left?"

The book alternates the story with italicized text about immigration and refugees. It would work nicely in the classroom to have one student read the roman text and one read the italicized text. The end of the book offers detailed information about Pol Pot, Ellis Island, refugees, and other topics covered in the book.

Stereotype-Busters

Point out to students that frequently discrimination is based on fear and on unfounded stereotypes. Make a chart on the bulletin board that lists stereotypes about different cultures. Then help students correct their stereotypes and write the reality in a second column. Discuss how stereotypes emerge. In what ways do they cause damage?

Further Reading: A teacher's guide is available for this book: *Who Belongs Here? Activity Guide*, by Margery Burns Knight and Thomas V. Chan. Send $12.95 to Tillbury House, Publishers, 132 Water Street, Gardiner, ME 04345.

Teaching Tip

Try to gauge the level of understanding in your class before you attempt this exercise. Although it can be valuable, it also has the potential to create awkward or hurtful situations. An example that could help them get started is: Stereotype: Japanese people wear kimonos. Reality: Kimonos are worn only on occasions to show traditional dress. Modern Japanese people dress much the way we do. Do not allow the discussion to digress into name-calling or laughing at the expense of one group.

LITERATURE LINK

A Very Important Day
by Maggie Rugg Herold
New York: Morrow Junior Books, 1995.

The Story: Set in New York City in late November, this story takes place over the course of one day. The reader sees different immigrants waking up and starting their days in different neighborhoods. The snowfall prompts them to remember things about their homelands as they prepare for this "very important day." Some take the subway, a bus, or a ferry, and an air of excitement builds. They are all heading to the same courthouse for a swearing in ceremony. Students will get a glimpse of the excitement and pride immigrants feel upon becoming citizens. The end of the book has a glossary and a fact sheet on citizenship.

Becoming a Citizen
Create a ceremony for your students to become citizens of your classroom. Start by making a list with them of what rights and responsibilities would be involved. Invite them to create a pledge of allegiance and an oath. You can follow the complete process: getting finger prints, taking applications, and giving tests. At the end, choose someone to preside over the ceremony.

WORKING TOGETHER

The Rights of the Child
The United Nations adopted the "Declaration of the Rights of the Child" to try to give children all over the world certain rights. Share the Declaration on page 78 with your students.

F•Y•I

Everyone shares his or her birthday with 10 million other people in the world.

The Greatest Table
by Michael J. Rosen
San Diego: Harcourt Brace & Company, 1994.

Background Information: This book was published in conjunction with Share Our Strength, an organization that helps the homeless. Proceeds from the book are used to fund shelters and school breakfast programs, and to fight hunger and poverty. The illustrators all donated their work. The author says, "Each illustrator's picture was to serve as a kind of ode or grace that would, likewise invite each reader to imagine a special place at this table for his or her own family." As your students read this book, ask them to think about the special role food plays in our culture, and in bringing people together.

The Book: Sixteen well-known children's illustrators, including Chris Van Allsburg, Floyd Cooper, and Diane Goode, have each donated a piece of art created to be one scene of a large dinner table. The pages fold together, accordion style, to form leaves of the table when opened. Each picture reveals a different part of our culture. Rosen's poem binds the text together, concluding:

F•Y•I

One in every eight American children under age 12 suffers from hunger.

The next time you sit down to eat,
The greatest table's set,
connecting you with each of us
who hasn't eaten yet.

So if you're hungry, join us here,
pull up another chair.
We'll all scoot over, make more room,
there's always some to spare.

Accordion Book

Students all over the country contributed to "the world's largest piece of children's artwork." Hundreds of classrooms submitted pages like the one shown here. Your students can make an accordion book like this one as well. Just take an 8 1/2 x 11" sheet of paper, divide into thirds as shown, and ask them to make the middle third be one leaf of the table. Invite them to think creatively—their table could be a picnic cloth or a cafeteria tray. Encourage them to represent their own culture in their panel. Then tape the pages of the accordion together with long strips of masking tape. On the back, have them write their names and any description or text they choose.

Name _____

Our National Symbols

Symbols are things that stand for other things. For instance, the Statue of Liberty stands for freedom in our country, and symbolizes our welcoming of new citizens. Our country has many symbols that help to unite our many and varied citizens. Some of them are shown below. What do they mean to you? Can you think of other symbols?

The stripes stand for the first thirteen states. The colors were chosen for their symbolism, too. Red stands for courage, white for purity, and blue for justice. What do the stars symbolize?

_____

_____

_____

What does the flag mean to you?

_____

_____

_____

Nicknames for the flag include "Old Glory;" "Stars and Stripes;" and "Star-Spangled Banner."

The bald eagle is our national symbol, chosen to represent freedom and courage.

But did you know:

• Benjamin Franklin argued that the turkey should be our national symbol. He thought the eagle was "a bird of bad moral character."

• Bald eagles are not bald! They have white feathers on their heads, which gives them a bald appearance.

• The nests of bald eagles weigh as much as a pick-up truck!

Find out more about bald eagles. Write two facts about them.

_____

_____

_____

_____

Name _____

Our National Symbols

On July 4th, 1776, people gathered in Philadelphia to hear the new Declaration of Independence read aloud. The Liberty Bell was rung to celebrate our new freedom. What words are engraved on this famous bell?

_____

_____

_____

_____

You have to go to Independence Hall to see the Liberty Bell. But you can see the Great Seal every time you look at a dollar bill. The olive branch in the eagle's talon symbolizes peace. What do these other details symbolize?

13 arrows _____

Note: Is the eagle looking in the direction of the olive branch or the arrows? Can you guess why?

_____

E Pluribus Unum _____

Design your own seal, symbolizing the qualities of our country that are important to you.

What My Symbol Means

_____

_____

_____

_____

_____

Name _____

Citizenship Test

Date _____

Country of Origin _____

Reason for Citizenship Request _____

_____

_____

What are the three branches of government?

_____

_____

_____

Which branch of the government has the offices of the President and Vice

President? _____

What do the stars and stripes on the United States flag represent?

_____

_____

What kind of government does the United States have?_____

What is the name of the President's official home?_____

Name one benefit of being a United States citizen. _____

Name one way that citizens can become informed voters.

_____

_____

_____

Where were the Declaration of Independence and the Constitution signed?

_____

Recite the Pledge of Allegiance.

Name _____

Citzenship Test

Match these quotations with the documents they're from.

___ 1. We the people of the United States . . ."

___ 2. "The citizens will elect . . ."

___ 3. "The mayor and city council will be the executive and legislative branches . ."

___ 4. ". . .freedom of religion, speech, press . . ."

___ 5. " . . .citizens 18 years or older can vote . . ."

___ 6. "As of April 3, 1988, first class letters need a 25¢ stamp."

___ 7. "Everyone must pass a driving test to get a license."

___ 8. "Three-fourths (3/4) of the states must vote to amend the Constitution."

a. Articles of the Constitution

b. Bill of Rights

c. Amendments 11-26

d. Preamble

e. a state constitution

f. a state law

g. a local charter

h. a federal law

Number Game

You need to remember some important numbers in the United States government. Fill in the blanks below with the correct numbers:

1. Number of branches in the United States Government   _____

2. Number of senators in the United States Congress   _____

3. Number of representatives in the United States Congress   _____

4. Number of Vice President(s) in the executive branch   _____

5. Number of Supreme Court Justices   _____

6. Number of states   _____

7. Number of amendments in the Bill of Rights   _____

8. George Washington was President number _____.   _____

9. In 1987, the Constitution was _____ years old.   + _____

Now add these numbers   = _____

Your answer has three numbers Each number represents a letter. Use the chart below. Find the numbers that form your answer and their matching letters.

0	1	2	3	4	5	6	7	8	9
S	E	P	D	O	T	L	R	U	A

Write the letters in the same order. You will see the name of a special place for you.

_____ _____ _____

Name _____

Declaration of the Rights of the Child

Being a citizen of the United States guarantees that people have certain basic rights. The United Nations adopted the "Declaration of the Rights of the Child" to try to give children all over the world certain rights. In 1990, over 150 nations signed the treaty. These shared rights—and our common responsibility to the world's children—are another way that we are all connected.

Principle One: We are the children of the world. No matter who our parents are, where we live, or what we believe, treat us as equals. We deserve the best the world has to give.

Principle Two: Protect us, so that we may grow in freedom and with dignity.

Principle Three: Let us each be given a name, and have a land to call our own.

Principle Four: Keep us warm and sheltered. Give us food to eat and a place to play. If we are sick, nurse and comfort us.

Principle Five: If we are handicapped in body or mind, treasure us even more and meet our special needs.

Principle Six: Let us grow up in a family. If we cannot be cared for by our own family, take us in and love us just the same.

Principle Seven: Teach us well, so that we may lead happy and useful lives. But let us play, so that we may also teach ourselves.

Principle Eight: In times of trouble, help us among the first. The future of the world depends on us.

Principle Nine: Protect us from cruelty and from those who would use us badly.

Principle Ten: As we grow up, we, too, will promote peace and understanding throughout the world.

What are some other principles you would like to see added to this list of children's rights?

_____

_____

_____

_____

_____

SELECTED BIBLIOGRAPHY

Lupita Manana
by Patricia Beatty
New York: William Morrow, 1981.

When I First Came to This Land
by Oscar Brand
New York: Putnam Publishing Group, 1965.

How Many Days to America? A Thanksgiving Story
by Eve Bunting
Boston: Houghton Mifflin, 1988.

We Came to America
by Frances Cavanagh
Philadelphia: Macrae Smith Company, 1954.

Gooseberries to Oranges
by Barbara Cohen
New York: Lothrop, Lee & Shepard, 1982.

Molly's Pilgrim
by Barbara Cohen
New York: Lothrop, Lee & Shepard, 1983.

Over Here It's Different: Carolina's Story
by Mildred Leinweber Dawson
New York: Macmillan Publishing Company, 1993.

A Very Important Day
by Maggie Rugg Herold
New York: Morrow Junior Books, 1995.

I'm New Here
by Bud Howlett
Boston: Houghton Mifflin Company, 1993.

Aldo Applesause
by Johanna Frank Hurwitz
New York: William Morrow, 1979.

Ellis Island: New Hope in a New Land
by William Jay Jacobs
New York: Charles Scribner's Sons, 1990.

Who Belongs Here?
by Margery Burns Knight
Gardiner, ME: Tilbury House Publishers, 1993.

Our National Symbols
by Linda Carlson Johnson
Brookfield, CT: The Millbrook Press, 1992.

Know Your Hometown History
by Abigail Jungreis
New York: Franklin Watts, 1992.

An Album of the Great Wave of Immigration
by April Koral
New York: Franklin Watts, 1992.

I Was Dreaming to Come to America
edited by Veronica Lawlor
New York: Viking, 1995.

In the Year of the Boar and Jackie Robinson
by Bette Bao Lord
New York: Harper & Row, 1984.

The Always Prayer Shawl
by Sheldon Oberman
Honesdale, PA: Boyds Mill Press, 1994.

My Fellow Americans: A Family Album
by Alice Provenson
San Diego: Browndeer Press, 1995.

I Speak English for My Mom
by Muriel Staneck.
Morton Grove, Illinois: Albert Whitman & Company,
1989.

The Whispering Cloth
by Pegi Deitz Shea
Honesdale, PA: Boyds Mills Press, 1995.

A Jar of Dreams
by Yoshiko Uchida
New York: Macmillan, 1981.

Angel Child, Dragon Child
by Mai Vo-Dinh
New York: Scholastic, 1983.

A Boat to Nowhere
by Maureen Crane Wartski
Philadelphia: Westminster John Knox, 1980.

A Long Way from Home
by Maureen Crane Wartski
Philadelphia: Westminster John Knox, 1980.

My Backyard History Book
by David Weitzman
Boston: Little Brown and Company, 1975.

*Tales From Gold Mountain: Stories of the Chinese
in the New World*
by Paul Yee
New York: Macmillan, 1989.

Encounter
by Jane Yolen
San Diego: Harcourt Brace & Company, 1992.

Cultures of America
series by Marshall Cavendish Corporation
North Bellmore, New York, 1995.

A World of My Own
series by Lodestar Books
New York: Dutton

American Voices
series by Rourke Corporation
Vero Beach, Florida, 1991

Answers to Worksheets

Page 74:   Flag: Stars symbolize the 50 states.

Page 75:   Liberty Bell: "Proclaim Liberty throughout all the land unto all the inhabitants thereof"- Leviticus 25:10

             Great Seal: 13 arrows symbolize 13 original states.

The eagle is looking toward the olive branch because it symbolizes peace.

E Pluribus Unum means "From many, one."

Page 76:   Branches of government: executive, legislative, and judicial.

Offices of President and Vice President are part of the executive branch.

Stripes represent the 13 original states; the stars represent the current states.

United States is a republic/representative democracy.

President lives in the White House.

Possible benefits of being a United States citizen are: the right to vote, freedom of speech, freedom of religion, equal treatment under the law, freedom of the press.

A few ways people can become informed citizens are by reading newspapers and magazines, listening to the news on the radio, or watching television news.

Declaration of Independence and the Constitution were signed in Philadelphia.

Page 77: Important Documents	Page 77: Number Game
1. d	1. 3
2. e	2. 100
3. g	3. 435
4. b	4. 1
5. c	5. 9
6. h	6. 50
7. f	7. 10
8. a	8. 1
	9. 200
	Total: 809

The special place spelled out is USA.